Wild Beasts and Angels

Wild Beasts and Angels

Remaining Human in the Healing Ministry

Michael Mitton

DARTON·LONGMAN+TODD

First published in 2000 by
Darton, Longman and Todd Ltd
1 Spencer Court
140–142 Wandsworth High Street
London SW18 4JJ

ISBN 0–232–52341–X

A catalogue record for this book is available from the British Library.

Designed by Sandie Boccacci
Phototypeset in 9½/13½pt Bookman by Intype London Ltd
Printed and bound in Great Britain by
Redwood Books, Trowbridge, Wiltshire

For my friends
who have faced the cold sickness of cancer
with wonderful faith, humanity, hope and humour:

Ian, Steve, Ros, John, Paul, John, Carol, Judy,
Ramon.

Contents

Foreword

I reflected lately that the Bible is such a strange and wonderful book as it has accompanied me down through the decades of my life and I have held it in my heart with all its fears and wonders. Michael Mitton has been sending me the chapters of *Wild Beasts and Angels* as he wrote them, and similar feelings of strangeness and wonder were evoked for me as I read them. I have found Michael to be a wonderful man in whom I have seen the love, light and healing mercy of God, and between us there continues to be evoked laughter and tears. Sometimes these tears are when I experience physical trembling and ecstasy in God, and sometimes the tears are when I suffer pain in my present weakness and vulnerability.

This very matter confronted me again as I read the last chapter of the story that goes alongside this book. I commend the book to you, and I look forward to reading it whole, and, with Michael, I stand in fear and trembling before the God with whom one day we shall be united eternally in fire and love.

Brother Ramon SSF
The Society of St Francis
Alleluia!

Introduction

The word 'healing' conjures up all kinds of images. To one, it will bring to mind a charismatic meeting. To another, it will be a contemplative prayer group; to another it will be a liturgical service with sacramental anointing; to yet others it will be a curious fringe activity for those who have nothing better to do, and for others still it will be something to do with herbal oils and soft music. Whatever kind of image comes to mind, most people see healing as something that you need when you are sick, and something that is done by trained people who know how to help sick people. Thus, when I have a fever, I call the expert doctor who comes complete with medical bag and heals me through a combination of knowledge, experience and medicine. Furthermore, if I am a Christian I may ask some fellow believers to come and pray for my healing, and I will again probably look to either the minister, or lay people trained for this task. In this way, the world of healing is focused around obvious sickness and is performed by 'experts'.

The more I consider this, the more uncomfortable I am with the dynamic. For a start, it misses the point that we are *all* sick to a greater or lesser degree. I have not met anyone who has not had some ailment, and certainly there is no one to my knowledge who does not have some inner psychological injury that still gives them pain. To some extent Western society is becoming aware of this, as more and more people give increasing attention to their fitness and health. Indeed the ever more prevalent 'health clubs' are not for the obviously 'unhealthy' – they are in the main for those who are in reasonable health who are seeking to maintain and improve their physical (and often mental) well-being. Health, rather like wealth, seems to have no limit – you can never have quite enough of it. Someone near you always seems to be that much healthier, have better skin tone, firmer muscles, brighter eyes and glossier hair. The great enemy for this health-conscious culture is ageing – that process that threatens to diminish physical health and thereby drain us of power. If the media is to be believed, it is the young and the beautiful who are the most valuable members of society. If it comes to the survival of the fittest, then the apparent survivors will be found in the gyms and beauty parlours. In many ways, secular society is very aware that we are all sick, so much so that it has made an obsession of health. And yet even the radiant young model in the hair gel advert will carry some measure of dis-ease. We live therefore with great discomfort with ill health. It is seen as a great enemy that must either be hidden or eliminated at all costs. Those who are sick are seen to be less useful in society – they have less power. Despite the marvellous advances in medicine, it is still a frightening thing to be sick in the Western world at the beginning of the new millennium.

From time to time we are made aware that even the powerful grow sick. The tragic accident of the American actor, Christopher Reeve, was somehow dreadfully symptomatic of our age. Here was the man who played the part of *Superman* – a superhero totally untouched by human disease and accident. Such was the exciting technology of the films, it almost seemed that Christopher Reeve himself could fly. 'After this, you will believe that man can fly' read the captions. But after this the actor fell from his horse and suffered the cruel blow of paralysis, and we saw on our TV sets not the flying superhero, but the powerless paraplegic. The actor's response to this terrible accident has been more genuinely heroic than that of the fictitious character he portrayed in the films, and he has certainly been saying something very significant to our culture about disability.

Again and again sickness and tragedy remind us of our own humanity and mortality, and our response to pain and sickness is to seek healing. The nature of our 'provider-client' society is that we nowadays instinctively look to the experts for help. When we are sick, we become clients of the healer. Increasing numbers of people are now paying private insurance policies for their health care and people want their money's worth. 'If I have paid all this out, I expect good service,' we may say, and great can be the anger if the healer is not able to deliver the goods. The sad valuing of all things by money only serves to make us more sick in spirit. So, the experts, who are often well paid (and the more expert you are, the more money you get, because you are more 'valuable'), come under increasing pressure to deliver the goods. When they fail to heal, it is usually they more than anyone who find it hardest to bear the failure.

Take this from the medical world to the world of church, and you find something similar. Many churches have considerable pastoral energy, so it is natural for them to want to care for the sick. Indeed, it is impossible to read the Gospels without wanting to reach out with the compassion and healing of Jesus to the sick. So, when someone gets sick, we send the 'expert' (the priest, pastor or trained lay person) and they do the job – usually, it has to be said, of comforting rather than providing any cure. Many people would testify to the enormous comfort this ministry does provide and that in itself makes the ministry immensely valuable. Sadly, of course, there are also stories of wounded and sick people going for the ministry of healing, and finding themselves reprimanded for their lack of faith and being abused in all manner of ways. When this happens, then the healing ministry has well and truly become sick, and the so-called healers are the most sick.

Thus, in the Christian world, healing again is seen to revolve around sickness. Healing is what we do when someone has an obvious sickness. This inevitably leads to a kind of 'bolt-on extra' mentality in church ministry. A church discovers it has sick people in it, so it sets about training healers. They are trained, and their ministry is bolted on to the other ministries in the church, and used accordingly. But I believe this compartmentalist view of healing is no longer so effective. For the healing ministry to have integrity and to be effective, it must be rooted in a spirituality of healing.

A spirituality for healing

Spirituality is right at the heart of our Christian life. It houses our beliefs, forms our behaviour, directs our relationship with God and others, helps us to understand ourselves in all our humanness, and helps us to make sense of our world. It is the engine room of our Christian lives. It is here that our deepest values are held. For a ministry of healing to be a natural part of our Christian lives, therefore, it has to be found in this engine room. Developing a spirituality of healing is about finding ways of making healing such a natural part of our human life that it will simply flow out from us instinctively. In this way it is entirely different from getting in the healing expert, or going into 'healing mode' when faced with a sick person. This does not mean to say that forms of training in the healing ministry are invalid. Far from it. It does say, however, that training in healing and health care will only be really effective when it comes naturally from our spirituality. Furthermore, those who find themselves particularly involved in the 'ministry of healing' will only do so effectively, if the whole community values healing as part of its corporate spirituality. This book, then, will explore how healing can move away from being perceived as the bolt-on extra for use with the sick, and can become a natural part of our personal and corporate spirituality. I hope it will be obvious from early on in this book that I understand spirituality to be a fundamental part of our humanity. It is not (as is sometimes portrayed) a polar opposite to our humanity. The activity of healing is one occasion where our spirituality and our humanity are very closely integrated.

As I gave thought to how to write this book, I struggled with the thought of it becoming a rather dull cerebral work. I found myself struggling against the predominant way in the West of presenting truth – with lots of words! I am a speaker and a writer and I am the first to admit that I speak and write long after there is nothing more to be said. Maybe one day I will be healed from this sickness that is endemic in my society. To balance this tendency, I have decided to introduce two other media into the book – *art* and *parable*.

- **Art**: I am so grateful to Lindsey Attwood who has produced a drawing for each chapter of the book. Some people will find they won't need to read much of my writing – Lindsey's drawings are far more articulate. I would strongly urge all readers to spend time with her drawings. I do believe God will speak to many through them.

- **Parable**: I have also introduced a parable, a story. In some parts of the world, story is a far more respected means of communication than it is in the West. Jesus himself taught in parables, and it is strange that we are often slow to follow his example. So I have had a go at writing a story. It is entirely fictitious. It will appear pathetically simple to some readers and rather unacademic. It will be transparently obvious what it is about, so it is not particularly clever. I have deliberately tried to avoid that experience that I have known in reading some fictitious writing, where I feel so totally left behind because I frankly cannot begin to understand what it is about. So I hope my simple story will be a rather more 'user-friendly' way of getting into this subject. It still uses words, but in a more economic and certainly less cerebral way.

The three media will all say the same thing. You may use all three, or you may simply want to use one or two. It is entirely up to you.

Spirituality and humanity

Finally, I have written this introduction on a day when I have received a letter from one of my dearest friends to tell me he has been diagnosed with cancer. This friend is Brother Ramon, who for the last eight years has lived the life of a hermit. Strangely, since his withdrawal I have felt much closer to him (and he to me). He has for me not only been a dear friend, but a prophetic figure, who with remarkable courage and humour, has been a fragile protest movement for peace, stillness and prayer in a world that is going insane with noise, activity and superficiality. As I write I feel dreadfully upset at the thought of my dear friend suffering, and possibly leaving this world far, far sooner than any of us would want. Ramon is the ninth close friend of mine in a short space of time to be assailed by this fearful disease. I write this book in gratitude for each of them: some of them have died, others are currently undergoing therapy, and others have come through the treatment and are cured of the disease. I have prayed for all of these, and have been involved in the laying on of hands for most of them. If healing is to do with curing, then I would have to say that my ministry of healing has been an abysmal failure.

But I am learning there is much more to healing than curing.

These friends of mine, some of whom have shared such deep wisdom through their pain, have helped me to see something more clearly about healing. I have experienced how vulnerable we feel in the face of illness and how much we long for healing. I know that death is the ultimate healing for those who are in Christ. I am in no doubt that each friend who has walked through the gates of Paradise has found peace at last, and they now know a joy that means they will never regret for one moment that they left this earth sooner than they wanted. However, I also know that untimely death is desperately painful for those left in the heartache of this world. Whichever way you look at it, there is something wrong about someone leaving this life too soon. I therefore cannot help but acknowledge that part of my humanity that has cried out so often these past three years, 'Dear God, please don't take this friend just yet.' In the face of serious sickness and death, healing prayer is raw, rather desperate, not usually very tidy and almost certainly not theologically respectable. But it is what happens in the extremes that often helps us to see what is happening in the normality. All sickness is puzzling and a little frightening. There is nothing romantic about either sickness or healing. We cry out to God in our pain because we are human and he is divine. We offer healing because we love our Lord Jesus who became human, bore our sicknesses and conquered death, and who has given us the blessed gift of the Holy Spirit to enable us to bring healing grace to our muddled lives here on earth.

We may understand little, but we are free to love much. It is in the face of death that we often discover just how much we love, and when we discover love, we are undoubtedly opening ourselves to God's healing presence in our lives. It is paradoxically this prayer for healing in the face of death, that causes me to pray for healing as a way of celebrating life. It is the future that makes sense of our present mortality. The future promise is of a healed soul *and* body that will dwell in the new heaven and new earth, and will worship the God who comes down to dwell among his people. The future vision is about perfect integration, and the gospel tells us that we may taste of that hope here and now. Healing, then, always has one eye on our future hope, but also is very conscious of the present. This book is an attempt to explore this integration of our humanity and spirituality, of our life and our death, of the mundane and the sublime, of the wild beasts and the angels.

> For her, no more the cruel snows of winter,
> The coldness and the fear in lonely night.
> No more the turmoil of the world around her
> But peace and light.
> For her no more bewilderment and sorrow
> No more the agony and stress of living
> And no more fears.
> For her, no more the grey of dying embers,
> A cheerless warmth breathed from a failing spark.
> For her the gold, the splendour and the glory;
> For us – the dark.

Written by my Aunt, Melody Collier, in 1976 after the death of her sister. Both sisters died of cancer.

Chapter 1

Following Jesus

In October 1997 I began work with the Acorn Christian Healing Trust. For eight and a half years prior to that I had worked as Director of Anglican Renewal Ministries. I faced, therefore, a shift of focus – from renewal to healing. This was not a big leap, for after all renewal and healing are close relatives. But starting this work with Acorn has given me the opportunity to explore the huge area of healing much more closely than was hitherto possible. And this exploration has been truly fascinating.

I was baptised as an infant in St John's Church, Edinburgh, and from that moment onwards I was never far from Anglican worship. At the age of seven my family moved south and I found myself worshipping at a small church in rural Buckinghamshire. As a child, my experience of church was of a very predictable routine of rather unintelligible yet comforting psalms, hymns, prayers and canticles, a short sermon from the vicar during which most in the congregation moved into a kind of transcendental slumber. The service was never longer than an hour and after slightly stilted conversations at the draughty church door we would return home to the welcome smells of Sunday lunch. I was not averse to this routine at all, but it seemed somewhat disconnected from my 'normal' world, and it certainly did not seem to offer any help to my childhood struggles, one of which was very irritating and at times acute eczema which broadened into asthma and hay fever during my teenage years. Nothing would have astonished me more if the vicar, one day, had offered to lay hands on me for healing. And yet, during those years in the 1960s and since then, thousands of churches, including both churches of my childhood, have developed regular healing ministries in which the sick have been invited to come forward for the laying on of hands.

I was ordained in 1978 and became Curate of St Andrew's Church, High Wycombe, a church that was in the full flush of charismatic renewal under the wise and kind leadership of John Hughes. John and I both enjoyed developing the healing ministry at this church. We were also part-time chaplains at Wycombe General Hospital. It was here that we tried to bring together the worlds of church and medicine. Early every Wednesday we would hold a service of Holy Communion in the little chapel with no visible congregation, yet with many patients listening through the hospital radio. As we then visited the wards carrying the sacrament, we saw something of a fusion between medical and spiritual care, as sick and injured souls reached out through their sick and injured bodies, and sometimes it was hard to tell which pain was the greater – the sickness in the soul or the body. Though the sacrament and the prayer for healing nearly always encouraged the soul, there were undoubtedly times when the physical body was affected as well and we would witness an accelerated recovery. The regular healing ministry in the church, and the frequent visits to the hospital enforced in me the conviction that healing was a fundamental part of Christian ministry.

During my last year at High Wycombe, the well-known church leader and evangelist David Watson came to lead a mission. David's humble and imaginative approach impressed me greatly. However, it was not long after I moved from Wycombe to become a team vicar in the parish of St George, Kidderminster, that I heard of David Watson's illness. Within the charismatic renewal movement there was tremendous concern for David, and considerable optimism that God would surely heal this man. However, in the cold February of 1984, news came through that he had died. This was a terrible blow for the charismatic renewal and for those of us within that movement who were also trying to encourage the ministry of healing. In many ways it exposed our superficiality. Surely, we supposed, if so many people pray for healing, God must answer? Our enthusiasm had led us to believe in worldly notions of power – when we meet things we dislike, then the way to deal with them is to exert ever increasing degrees of force applied by as many as possible. Thousands of Spirit-filled Charismatic praying throughout the world would surely be sufficient to prevent a Christian leader from dying so young. And yet, despite all that prayer, David died. Some supposed that David's death was due to lamentable lack of faith in the Church. Others put it down to spiritual warfare – that the devil was prowling around like a roaring lion and had found someone to devour. Thankfully there were some who were prepared to probe the deeper mysteries of suffering, and David Watson himself led the way in this in writing his impressive book, *Fear No Evil.*[1]

The healing ministry in the charismatic renewal at that time might have been dealt a very serious blow. However, during the last few years of his life, David Watson had made very close friends with the Californian church leader, John Wimber, whose healing ministry was very impressive. In some ways, David's parting gift to the renewal movement was to draw our attention to John Wimber, for in the years that followed, Wimber was to become an enormous influence on the charismatic renewal in the life of the Church. He had a wonderful honesty about his struggles in the ministry of healing, but though he acknowledged that there were many unsolved mysteries in this ministry, it was none the less not difficult to go to a sick person and pray for healing.

When I was a vicar in Kidderminster in the West Midlands, we were greatly encouraged by Graham Dow (now Bishop of Willesden) visiting our church with a team from his parish church in Coventry and teaching many of us to engage in the ministry of healing following the guidelines developed by John Wimber. After this, we were training many people to be engaged in offering prayer for healing, not only at the Communion rail during a healing service, but in their homes, places of work, even in the check-out queue at Tesco's! It was a radical development in the healing ministry, for healing was seen now not simply as the reserve of 'specialist healers', but was actually a part of normal discipleship in which many could engage. Slowly it was dawning on me that healing was not just an optional extra for people who liked that sort of thing – it was a gift of our generous God available to all who sought to serve him in a world of suffering and sickness.

When I became Director of Anglican Renewal Ministries I found on my desk a manuscript of a new course on the healing ministry, written by Revd Roger Vaughan. In a short time this became the very popular *Saints for Healing*, which has encouraged thousands to engage in the ministry of healing. In the many meetings and services that I visited during my time with Anglican Renewal Ministries, I saw many different expressions of the healing ministry, and found increasingly it was being welcomed in the life and ministry of the Church. I also became very aware that the healing ministry was fast growing in other traditions. For example, the ministry of healing is an integral part of the Catholic spirituality of Walsingham, and it plays an important part in the ecumenical spirituality of the Celtic-inspired Iona Community, to name but only two. Also the faithful ministry of the Churches' Council of Health and Healing, the Guild of St Raphael, and the Guild of Health were also doing excellent work in bringing the ministry of healing to the attention of churches of all denominations. We are now approaching that point where the ministry of healing is becoming widely accepted in the Church. All the denominational Churches now have regional healing advisers and thousands of churches have incorporated healing into the ongoing ministry of the church.

The more popular use of the ministry of healing should mean therefore that we are getting better at it. If more churches are engaging in the ministry of healing, then surely there should be fewer sick people around.

However, my impression is that this is not the case. Despite the increase of interest in the ministry of healing, churches are still finding themselves encountering those painful puzzles that were faced so publicly when David Watson was ill: we pray for people who are sick, but in many instances they still remain sick; we pray for the sick, and in many instances they not only remain sick, but they die an untimely death. The ministry may be growing, but the puzzles are not diminishing. Our task therefore is not only to encourage the ministry of healing, but also to develop a spirituality that is able to contain the considerable puzzles that present themselves through this ministry.

This is the aim of this book, and my starting point is to look at the example of our Lord Jesus who engaged in a most spectacular healing ministry that not only involved healing thousands of sick people of all kinds of diseases, but included also delivering people from the influence of demons, and, on occasions, praying for people who had died, and bringing them back to life and to full health. Not only did Jesus engage in this ministry, but he trained his disciples to follow his example, and the infant church duly found itself praying for the sick and it saw them healed. What happened, therefore, in the heart and soul of Jesus and his disciples that enabled them to engage in this ministry of healing? I believe we must begin with a study not of the divinity of Jesus, which would seem an obvious place to find the resources of divine healing, but of the humanity of Jesus, for it is there that I find some important clues about this ministry.

Jesus and the Spirit

The inspiration for this book came to me at the beginning of the season of Lent. I found myself again back in the familiar story of the temptation of Jesus in the wilderness. Mark's version of the story is this:

> John the baptizer appeared in the wilderness, proclaiming a baptism of repentance for the forgiveness of sins. And people from the whole Judean countryside and all the people of Jerusalem were going out to him, and were baptized by him in the river Jordan, confessing their sins. Now John was clothed with camel's hair, with a leather belt around his waist, and he ate locusts and wild honey. He proclaimed, 'The one who is more powerful than I is coming after me; I am not worthy to stoop down and untie the thong of his sandals. I have baptized you with water; but he will baptize you with the Holy Spirit.'
>
> In those days Jesus came from Nazareth of Galilee and was baptized by John in the Jordan. And just as he was coming up out of the water, he saw the heavens torn apart and the Spirit descending like a dove on him. And a voice came from heaven, 'You are my Son, the Beloved; with you I am well pleased.' And the Spirit immediately drove him out into the wilderness. He was in the wilderness for forty days, tempted by Satan; and he was with the wild beasts; and the angels waited on him. Now after John was arrested, Jesus came to Galilee, proclaiming the good news of God. (Mark 1:4–14)

Mark begins his Gospel with this dynamic figure of John who is to be found in the wild Judean desert, and who is proclaiming a baptism for the forgiveness of sins. It is an extraordinary renewal movement which was taking place not in the fertile plains, but in the barren desert lands. John is not equipped with tent and travelling team, moving from city to city. He is living in solitude in the wilderness, and thousands are pouring out of the towns and cities to go and hear him preach in the desert. If you were living in Judea at that time, to get to hear him, you had to leave the comforts of your home, take time off your work, and trudge into the dusty desert feeling the burning sun by day, and the chilly air at night. The very journey itself would prepare you for your encounter with John, for as you walked among the sand and dust and stones, you would become aware of your own inner barrenness and spiritual emptiness. And then, after a time, you would find John, dressed strangely, and if you found him eating, you would have seen him chewing at honey-coated wild locusts. It was a fairly unpromising setting for a renewal, and yet a renewal it was, for thousands and thousands flocked into the desert, and in it was John who helped them discover that the desert could be holy ground, a place of encounter with the living God, a place of purging of conscience, of repentance of sin.

The image that was of course so dramatically powerful in this desert place, was the river Jordan, the main river of Israel that flows from Mount Hermon in the far north and passes through Lake Huleh and Lake Galilee on its winding journey down to the Dead Sea. The name 'Jordan' means 'the descender' and it does indeed descend a long way as it flows through the deepest rift valley on earth. As it passes through Lake Huleh it is

230 ft above sea level, but by the time it reaches the Dead Sea it is 1,290 ft below sea level. In the north it passes through rich fertile lands, but as it approaches the Dead Sea it passes through the Judean wilderness, and its presence provides a thin band of green jungle in an otherwise dry land.

So John baptises people in the Descender. They come, descend into the water where they die to their sinful lives, and rise again to new life. Then, one day, John, probably in the midst of his baptising, sees Jesus coming to the waters. The evangelist, John, tells us that as the Baptiser sees Jesus coming he says, 'Behold the Lamb of God, who takes away the sin of the world.' There must have been some present who felt anxious about this. A Lamb in the wilderness? The wilderness would not be a safe place for a lamb. It's striking that John should choose such a vulnerable image, and he does not even try and strengthen the image by calling him the Ram of God, or the Great Sheep of God. No, this is the *Lamb* of God, and in time this Lamb would come to another river, the river of death, where he would be the Lamb led to the slaughter to offer his life as the sacrifice for all sin. But here, Jesus engages in the symbolic act of baptism, identifying with fallen humanity. And the crowds watch while John baptises Jesus.

There must have been much that was puzzling for the crowds about this event. For a start, John hails Jesus as the one who is to take away the sins of the world. Furthermore, he is one, mightier than John, on whom the Spirit will rest, and he is the one who will baptise with the mighty Holy Spirit and with fire. For those first hearers, their expectations must have been sky high.

And yet John was pointing to an apparently normal human being like himself. Those from Nazareth might well have recognised him as Joseph's lad. How could a local carpenter take away the sins of the world? Right away, we are beginning to grasp that this Saviour figure is remarkably human like us. In fact he is disturbingly like one of us, and for those who wanted a superhuman hero figure, this would have been something of a disappointment. But then something extraordinary does happen: for when Jesus comes up for air, we are told that the heavens are torn apart, and the onlookers and first readers are now reassured – this is someone who really is in touch with heaven, so much so that a voice comes from heaven proclaiming him as a much-loved son. But something else strange happens: a dove appears from nowhere and descends towards Jesus, and we are told this was the Holy Spirit coming upon Jesus. This dove is highly significant.

Some years ago I was asked to preach at a Pentecost Praise service in Salisbury Cathedral, and I decided to preach on this passage. In my preparations for this service, I became increasingly fascinated by the fact that all four of the evangelists tell us that the Spirit came upon Jesus as a dove, and Luke adds 'in bodily form'. The dove has always been a significant image in Scripture, but somehow I felt the evangelists were saying that there was something important about the physicality of the expression of the Spirit in this story. I became intrigued by this dove, and found that in the Greek the word is a female word, *peristera*. After a bit of research I discovered this word was used for the rock dove, which is not your white fluffy-looking creature that graces that great painting of the baptism of Jesus by Piero della Francesca, but a rather dull-looking bird, more like our well-known wood pigeon. There is a disappointing ordinariness about this bird. But I was interested then to research an ornithological guide to find out a bit more about this rock dove. In David Bannerman's *Birds of the British Isles* (Vol. 8), he writes, 'It is a rock frequenting bird, never perching on trees. It has however been known under special circumstances to alight upon water'. This felt very relevant. As I read on, I discovered that the rock dove's natural habitat was the desert, and therefore it is not surprising that this was the creature to alight on the baptised Jesus. But I was even more interested to read further about its nesting habits, described in the same volume by Henry Graham, a naturalist of Iona, who writes in a wonderful poetic way about the nesting places of the rock dove in the Scottish islands:

> Many of these caverns are horribly gloomy and forbidding – deep black dens extending far beyond the reach of the light of day, stretching into the very bowels of the admantine cliff; the air smells dank and foul, and the walls are dripping with unwholesome slime. Such caves generally have legends attached to them – of a fugitive clansman hiding from the pursuit of the avenger of blood, of wholesale deeds of murder, or of wild scenes of diablerie; and the names of the 'Cave of Death', the 'Pit of Slaughter' and the 'Hobgoblin's Den' are often met with, showing their grim character. These haunts of bygone murderers, smugglers and outlaws, are now tenanted by doves, the emblem of innocence.[2]

The rock dove delights to frequent such inhospitable and dark places, and there she transforms them by turning them into places of life. It is an image of the Spirit that has become my favourite. This is no white fluffy creature beautifying Christian meetings, but is a rugged creature that delights to transform the desperate and dark places of our broken world, making them places of new life. It is also interesting to note that this is a female image of the Spirit, embracing both courage and tenderness, which tells us something about the feminine in the Godhead.

Mark tells us that as this physical dove alights upon Jesus, at the same time the heavens are 'torn apart'. He uses this word (*schizo*) twice in his Gospel: here, and in chapter 15 verse 38 where he tells us that, at the time of Jesus' death, 'the curtain of the temple was *torn* in two, from top to bottom'. In other words, here at the baptism of Jesus, there is a healing of the divide between heaven and earth which corresponds to that great healing that takes place at the Cross. The heavens are torn open in the same way as the curtain dividing the people from the Holy of Holies was torn open at the time of Jesus' death. And at the heart of this most wonderful healing comes the voice of love: 'You are my beloved Son, in whom I am well pleased.' In the person of Jesus dwells the human and the divine, and his very presence on earth demonstrates that the love of God has, as it were, broken out of heaven and invaded earth. Now, secure in the knowledge that he is loved, the human divine Jesus goes out into the wilderness.

It was this Spirit who drove Jesus into the wilderness. Mark uses the word *ekballo*, a word of some force from which we get the word 'ballistic' as in a missile. With power, the rock dove Spirit drove Jesus into her natural habitat, and it was here that Jesus discovered some dark caves indeed.

Jesus and the wilderness

We now have this mysterious scene of the divine yet human Jesus being driven into the wilderness place. He becomes immensely vulnerable again, as vulnerable as the baby in the stable at Bethlehem. Now he is a lamb in the wilderness, made weaker by having no physical sustenance. His mortal frame weakened, he has to face not only the rigours of the wilderness, but also the fierce temptations of Satan. And yet he is unmoved and ultimately triumphant. Mark tells us that 'He was in the wilderness forty days, tempted by Satan; and he was with the wild beasts; and the angels waited on him' (1:13). When I first meditated on this verse, it was as though with my mind's eye I could see Jesus in the wilderness. I saw that inhospitable Judean landscape of dust and sand and rocks, and I could see the Lord Jesus sitting on a rock. On one side of him I saw the wild beasts, creatures that would normally destroy and devour weaker life forms like humans. Somehow in this image I could see that they were still wild and yet subdued by being in the presence of Jesus. They co-existed without having to devour. On the other side I saw one of heaven's glorious angels caring for him.

I find this is a highly symbolic image. We see Jesus, right at the outset of his public ministry, being at ease with both the earthly and the divine. He is at ease with the wilderness with its wild beasts. During this testing period in particular, he is facing the stark reality of the broken and sinful world in which he is living. The wild beasts are wild because there is wildness in the world, a wildness that is connected to the fallenness of the human race and the appalling exile from that first garden. The desert speaks of fallen creation. There should be verdant life on earth, but instead there are rocks, dust and stones. There should be peace on earth, but there is violence. There should be justice on earth, but there is repression and poverty. And Jesus is made terribly aware of the fallen state of the world during these days, the world that he helped to create. But not only does he face the wild beasts without during these days in the wilderness; he also has to face the wild places within his own soul – the places of temptation.

In this wilderness place he is facing the great adversary of humankind – the Beast, Satan – and Satan's strategy to bring down Jesus is sinister – he goes for the human nature in which the divine Son of God dwells. Jesus is made to feel the intensity of human temptation. In these days he faces the full horror of what fallen humanity is capable, and he faces it not in his encounters with fallen people, but in the closets of his own human frame. In those six weeks in the wilderness, Jesus, fully Son of God, was discovering the full force of what it meant to be human, and the fiery trials that threaten human life. We know he never gave in to sin, yet he knew the power of temptation. The wild beasts therefore are symbolic of the potentially chaotic and destructive both in our world and in our humanity. In the company of Jesus, we find these wild beasts are at peace and no longer threaten.

Supporting Jesus in all of this are the angels, creatures normally unseen to the human eye, yet creatures
that feature regularly in Bible stories, and in church
tradition. They are sinless, pure, wonderful creatures of
heaven who assist us on earth. Mark uses the word
diakone to describe how the angels were assisting
Jesus. They were being deacons to Jesus, a word normally associated with serving at tables, which is an irony
as Jesus is fasting in this wilderness. It makes me think
of that question in Psalm 78:19, 'Can God spread a table
in the wilderness?', and the answer here is 'most definitely yes!' On this table, however, is not ordinary food.
The angels are feeding a different food to him, the food of
heaven, for 'humankind cannot live by bread alone, but
by every word that proceeds from the mouth of God'
(Matt. 4:4). I sometimes wonder how they ministered
to Jesus, and my guess is that they were reminding him
of the words that Jesus had so recently heard from
the mouth of God, 'You are my beloved Son, in whom
I am well pleased.' It was the knowledge that he was
loved by his Father that gave Jesus the inner security to
acknowledge and face the wild beasts of his humanity.

Thus it is that in this wilderness the lion lies down
with the Lamb – a truly remarkable and unthinkable
event, yet it happens. The coming of Jesus into our
world brings such hope to broken humanity. Luke tells
us that Jesus returned from this time in the wilderness
'filled with the power of the Spirit'. It is fascinating to
see that the way to be filled with the power of the Spirit
is to explore the depths of our humanity. Having arrived
at his home town of Nazareth, Jesus goes to the syna-

gogue and reads the passage from Isaiah which proclaims,

> 'The Spirit of the Lord is upon me,
> because he has anointed me to bring good news to the poor.
> He has sent me to proclaim release to the captives and recovery of sight to the blind,
> to let the oppressed go free,
> to proclaim the year of the Lord's favour.' (Luke 4:18f.)

The rock dove Spirit is upon him, and will now take him to the dark caves of human suffering to bring the gospel of light. It is interesting to see that the moment he announces this, someone says, 'But isn't this Joseph's son?' (Luke 4:22). It is the very humanity of Jesus which is an offence to people. There is a feeling of 'Who is he to tell us what to do – he is one of us'. They are unable to comprehend that within this human there is the divine Son of God. For them, the Messiah must be high and exalted, untarnished by the dust and grime of this wild world. And yet it is precisely because Jesus is 'one of us' that he is able to achieve all he does. In the coming three years, Jesus will travel through the towns and villages of Galilee, Judea and beyond, and he will encounter the wild beasts of sickness, fear, anger, anguish, injustice, cruelty and much more. He will also meet the wild beast of death at Calvary so that even that beast will cease to be an enemy.

It is the example of our Lord Jesus that provides for me a starting point for the ministry of healing, for it is he who shows us what it means to be truly human, a humanness that is also filled with the Spirit. A little while ago I was asked to write a meditation on the wilderness, and I used the story of the temptations of Jesus.

WALKING IN OUR WILDERNESS

Too strong the burning sun
Scorching straining plants
making rocks too hot to touch,
rocks that look like loaves of bread
yet cannot fill an empty stomach.
The Son of Man looks upon the rocks
and feels the empty stomach
and knows the longings of his humanity.

Too grand the kingdoms of the world
from this high place.
kingdoms of wealth and power
but power that is like sand in the wilderness
empty, unable to give the waters of life.
The Son of Man looks upon the kingdoms
and sees the foolish promises of glory
and knows the weakness of his humanity.

Too high the pinnacle of this Temple.
How much does a Father delight in his son?
Is he so well pleased,
that he would stretch out his hand
and catch his falling child?
The Son of Man looks down from the vertiginous
height

and sees the hard rocks below
and feels the fears of his humanity

The Son of Man stills himself in the place of worship
and hears again the voice of his Father
"You are my Beloved Son.
You are my much beloved Child"

In the wasteland
The voice of hope echoes in dark caves
    and jagged mountain tops
that waters *shall* flow in the wilderness
and sifted sand shall bring forth fragrant flowers,
For God has taken this dry and broken humanity
and with the verdant voice of love
has brought forth life in us!

Story part 1:

The man who thought
he was wise

It was a Monday when the man who thought he was wise read about the blind girl.

She lived far away from his world in a land of poverty. The man who thought he was wise, also thought he was wealthy, though not as wealthy as his younger brother, and on dark days he would look longingly at his brother's wealth. But the man who thought he was wise and reasonably wealthy felt he had almost enough, and he looked upon his well-kept semi-detached suburban house, and his new Ford Sierra, and his three-piece suite bought for less than £2000 in a great sale, and his microwave oven that saved him so much time, and his state of the art sound system that helped him relax, and his four TV sets with videos, two downstairs and two up, and his CD-ROM Internet-friendly computer which opened the whole world up to him, and he smiled with contentment. Yet he felt bad about the poor girl that he had come across on his Internet. She was blind and had none of these things, and therefore she was poor indeed.

So the man who thought he was wise decided to go to the girl who was blind and poor, for he knew he could share with her his wealth, and pray for her health, for he believed in the power of prayer. He set out on his journey, and he loaded his Ford Sierra with every provision to sustain him on his long journey, for he did not want to be hungry like the poor girl. His eyes were bright as he locked up his house and embarked on his journey. 'This is the wisest thing I've done,' thought the man who thought he was wise.

For five weeks the man who thought he was wise drove across foreign lands until the sun burned hot, and the people's skins grew dark, and it became harder to find cash machines that would turn his card into cash, hard-earned cash, though not as much as his brother. In the fifth week he arrived in the wilderness, and to the man who thought he was wise, this was indeed a wild place. It was here that his Ford Sierra failed, and it was here that he found himself walking among the rocks and thorns of the wild place on his way to help the girl who was poor and blind. The man who thought he was wise sat down in the wilderness, beneath the shade of a juniper tree and watched the dancing air above the scorched tarmac road, the road that led to the village where lived the girl who was poor and blind.

As evening fell he heard the roars of the beasts of the wilderness, and he felt fear in his chest like he had never known before. It was frightening to see strange, sinister shapes – trees and rocks, once venerated by primitive peoples, once seen to be the habitation of dark spirits. But worse still for the man who thought he was wise, were those moments when he looked into the wilderness of his own soul, and discovered wild beasts that he had been too blind to see. Dark and sinister were the shapes within, and he wondered whether they were the habitation of dark spirits.

In the darkest hour of the night, the man who thought he was wise came to the knowledge that he had no wisdom, and he wept himself to a disturbed sleep with disturbed dreams. Then in the midst of a wild dream, a messenger of light appeared, an undefined, undefiled creature of grace, who ministered unto him.

The man who knew he had no wisdom awoke as the massive sun heaved itself up over the far-off mountains, shedding its light and heat over the night-rested wilderness. Into the silence of dawn came a sound, the sound of a motorbike. Thus it was that he continued his journey on the back of a bike, behind a young man with dark skin, whose language he knew not. Although the man knew he was no longer wise, he knew he could still help the girl who was blind and poor, and his spirits rose as he journeyed through the wilderness, not far now from his destination.

Chapter 2

Healing and Humanity

Towards the end of the fourth century AD there was a growing debate in the Church about the nature of our humanity. The debate essentially centred around the question of whether humans were intrinsically evil or good. When we are born into this world, is our natural inclination to evil or to good? In the West, the theologian, Ambrose, was arguing that all humans sinned in Adam. Adam was corrupted by sin and his descendants were inevitably infected with sin. Thus, all of us are sinners because we inherit Adam's sin, and thereby even a day-old child is a sinner. He also taught that added to this inherited sin is our personal sin. The Greek fathers in the East, however, had a more optimistic outlook on human nature. The Gregories of Nazianzus and Nyssa, along with John Chysostom, taught that newborn children were sinless. Though human nature was prone to sin, it did have free will. The debate reached a crescendo with the great theologian, Augustine of Hippo. The issue hinged on what happened at Adam's fall from grace in the Garden of Eden. Augustine followed Ambrose in teaching that once Adam became infected with sin, so did every human thereafter. Augustine picked up the teachings of some before him that, as a result of this infection, all infants were sinful even in their mother's womb, and they needed baptism and exorcism to rescue them. Without baptism, they would pass to the eternal fire (though Augustine conceded that their suffering would be less than that of adults). Also like others before him, Augustine believed that the taint was propagated from parent to child by the physical act of generation. The carnal excitement that went with the sex act was, according to Augustine, a sure sign of this. All humans therefore instinctively carry the symptoms of this sickness, the most severe being ignorance, concupiscence and, of course, death. In Augustine's understanding, 'concupiscence' stands for that tendency in humans to turn from the spiritual to the material, and Augustine does make clear that in his opinion the most widespread and dangerous of these is sexual desire. According to Augustine, it was because of this that Jesus chose to be born of a pure virgin. In Augustine's view, the whole of humanity is a 'lump of sin' (*massa peccati*), destined for everlasting damnation, but rescued from it by Christ.

Augustine faced a strong opponent to his doctrine, namely the British Celt, Pelagius, who was a teacher of theology in Rome until 409 AD. Pelagius was shocked by Augustine's views of human nature, which he considered demoralising and far too pessimistic. The fact that humans could not help sinning seemed to Pelagius to be an insult to the Creator. He rejected Augustine's view that humans have an intrinsic bias towards wrongdoing. He believed that each soul was created by God and, regardless of his or her parents, was born good and undefiled, unsoiled by original sin inherited from Adam.

He acknowledged that Adam's sin was certainly disastrous, and was clear that humankind needed the saving grace of Christ.[1]

No doubt the fierce conflict between Pelagius and Augustine pushed them into more extreme positions. In the end Augustine was the clear victor, and Pelagius was the heretic, and the Western, pessimistic view of human nature has prevailed in most of the Western Church since then. The Church's fear of human sexuality is one obvious symptom of this inheritance. However, in the East and in the Celtic Church the suspicions of human nature were far less severe. In this respect, they were true to the Jewish roots of the Church. Part of me wonders whether the Western Church's suspicion of human nature was in reaction to the Jewish celebration of human nature. Anti-semitism was rife in the Church from a very early stage. By and large the Church adopted Latin and Greek forms of thinking and abandoned the earthy creation-affirming approach of its Jewish heritage.

The Western Church was influenced by Latin and Greek philosophy from an early stage. The Greeks feared passions, believing them to be impersonal forces that could possess individuals and cause them to lose control. Homer's heroes interpreted passions as direct workings of demons. *Reason* was highly prized and was regarded as the superior quality in the human, whereas emotions were inferior. For the Stoics, reason and emotion were sharply contrasted. Emotions belonged to the animal nature in humanity, and reason to the divine in humanity. God therefore was full of reason, but could not contain any emotion.

One of the consequences of this suspicion of human nature was a profound unease with human passions and emotions which represents a considerable departure from the doctrine of humanity as seen in the Old Testament and as celebrated in Jewish spirituality. Whereas the Western Church was propounding the view that passions are disturbances or weaknesses of the soul, we find that the human followers of God in the Old Testament are people who could be filled with righteous rage, weep with open displays of sorrow, laugh and celebrate with food and wine, and appreciate the fullness of sexual joy between the lover and the beloved, as expressed in the Song of Solomon (which the Church turned into an allegory of Christ and the Church, as it had great difficulty in accepting an erotic love song in its Scriptures). All this celebration of the goodness of human nature was in the context of serving a God who hated sin, and was intolerant with anger that became violent crime, celebration that became debauchery and love that became lust. Humans were entrusted with passions to use them rightly.

The sad divide between Jewish and Christian spirituality has had terrible consequences for the Church. But as writers like Michele Guinness have shown, there is no difficulty in expressing our Christian life in the framework of the Jewish spirituality in which our faith was birthed.[2] Had we kept true to our inheritance, we would have had a far healthier view of human nature, one which fully celebrated its goodness and was realistic about its weaknesses. I can't help feeling that had we followed this path, we would have had a far healthier Church through the ages. Furthermore, a Church that has persistently communicated to humans that they are worthless sinners is now reaping the reward of an inevitable reaction. This is an age, more than any, when people need to be valued in their whole humanity. The good news is that I see a shift taking place in the Church in which we are providing safe places where we can acknowledge the shadow side of our humanity and own up to the presence of the wild beasts within us, without fear of condemnation from our fellow believers. We are also discovering that there are beasts within us which, far from being destructive, are actually a God-blessed part of our humanity.

Owning our humanity

During those testing days in the wilderness our Lord Jesus learned to face the wild beasts, and part of his reason for that was to provide a way for us to follow. For it was he who showed us how to live a fully human life. If we are to look for an example of one who is fully human, then we need to look no further than the pages of the Gospels. And we find a human who is not stoic, prizing reason over emotion, but one who demonstrates the full range of human passion and emotion, as well as the wonderful skills of reason.

The way of life that Jesus taught was not one of escapism from being human. The early heresy of Manichaeism (that at one time influenced Augustine) taught that all matter was intrinsically evil, and all spirit was good. Regularly the Church has fallen into this trap of thinking that the way of getting closer to God is to deny the material life and invest solely in the spiritual life. The fact is that there are blessings and dangers in both the material and spiritual worlds. Jesus taught clearly about the perils within both. For example, to the woman who was caught in the act of adultery, he made clear that her act was wrong and he cautioned her not to sin again. But he also addressed another more serious dimension that was not so obvious, and this was to do with what was going on inside the condemning men. Although the men were not actually engaged in the material act of adultery, their attitudes of superiority and hypocrisy were equally as sinful as adultery. In fact, you get the impression in the story that theirs is the more serious crime.

How had Jesus become so astute? Surely it was because during those testing days in the wilderness, and at other times in his life, he had dared to explore his own soul, the soul of a grown man with normal male desires. He had found such desires in his own soul, and rather than retreating from them or trying to hide them he was prepared to face them. He knew that his calling was to singleness and, like anyone called to the celibate life, he had to search his own humanity and work out the implications of this for his life. In the searchings of his humanity, he discovered the potential for men to abuse women sexually, the fantasies that degenerate, the defence mechanisms that would judge others as a way of avoiding a proper attention to sinful or wounded places in our own soul. Jesus showed such a clear understanding of human nature that there is no way he fostered a spirituality that was about disconnecting spirit and body. What he did discover was a wisdom that could assess what, among the many and varied wild beasts of humanity, were healthy and creative, and what were destructive and abusive. All this was in the context of being beloved by his Father in heaven.

Pastorally, so much damage has been done through the ages because of the grim suspicion of human nature. Whether it be in a convent school or an evangelical prayer group, talk to many Christian people and they will tell tales of profound anxiety because of what was communicated to them about their own humanity. But I sense a new gentleness appearing in many parts of the Church, which is not least to do with daring to face our humanity, to welcome it into the love of God for his affirming, healing and, where necessary, his correction. The last forty years has seen a mushrooming of Christian counselling, and ministries of inner healing and healing of the memories. This speaks of a willingness to explore our humanity and face whatever beasts we may find within, in the context of the safety of God's love which is unconditional, and certainly not put off by human nature.

The beginning of the healing journey

How we view our humanity will very much affect how we do our healing ministry. The more I reflect on the ministry of healing with all its joys, sorrows and mysteries, the more I am convinced that a spirituality for healing is located in the spirituality of the desert. It is in the desert that we are brought face to face with the wild beasts within and without, and we are made aware of the miraculous resources of heaven. The desert is the place of triumph and testing, of weary perseverance and unexpected revelation, of training in disciplines and discoveries of freedom. So what does this mean in practice for the ministry of healing? A spirituality of healing based in desert spirituality will mean that I am at ease with my full humanity, composed as it is of a rich mixture of flesh, blood, spirit, emotions, memories, relationships, environment and so on. It is in this realm that I will experience the pain and dysfunction that causes me to seek for healing. Reflect for a moment on the story of Peter: Peter discovers a swelling in his abdomen. A visit to the doctor and subsequent investigations give him the grim news that he has a cancer in his stomach. Peter is a Christian and he becomes aware of a whirlwind of responses going on within him. In his body he is aware of discomfort and swelling, and weariness; in his emotions he is aware of fear and dread; in his reason he is aware of a hundred and one practical plans needed to adjust to this illness and possible death; in his spirit he is aware of God, mysterious yet loving.

Enter Earnest, keen Christian and fervent reader of Christian healing books. He is in no doubt that God will heal Peter. What Peter must not do is to give into the demon doubt. He is a child of God who must stand firm on the promises of God. God has done many mighty healings before, and he can do one for Peter. If Peter feels pain he must recognise it as a work of the enemy and rebuke it in Jesus' name; if he feels fear he must destroy it with faith; if he doubts that God can heal, he must put his trust in the word of God. Peter will get well, not by the drugs and treatments of the secular doctors, but by the miracle-working power of prayer. In fact God might well want him to throw the pills away.

Peter is also visited by another friend, Jim, who like Earnest is a Christian, but a rather different kind. He

feels himself to be much enlightened by those theologians who have shaken off the shackles of naive
thinking. When he visits Peter he is compassionate but
downcast. He hears the news that the prognosis is poor.
He shakes his head as he looks at Peter and is keen to
know what the medical world can do to help. He talks
awkwardly about God and uses difficult language that
does not make any sense to Peter. He assures Peter
that God does not intervene with the miraculous, but he
will provide comfort.

Peter feels depressed by both visitors. After Earnest
leaves, he feels he will never have enough faith to get
the healing he so wants. Earnest has failed to listen to
his fears and anxieties, and if he did tell Earnest about
them, he would surely receive a rebuke for having insufficient faith. After Jim leaves Peter feels that God is
complicated and powerless.

The characters may be parodies, but there are many
in the Church who would recognise these two
approaches. One is at home with the angels but nervous
of the wild beasts, and the other is suspicious of angels
but at ease with the wild beasts. The 'patient' is not
particularly helped by either, not least because the
visitors are keener to bolster their theological point than
be a true friend. So what is the appropriate response?

The healing journey has to begin not with defending
a theological position, nor flights into spiritual fantasy-
land, but it has to begin with something much more
down to earth. The journey has to begin with honesty –
an honest response to human pain and struggle. When
we encounter a friend who is sick, we will firstly need
to listen to what is going on inside our own humanity.

When, in August 1998, I received the letter from my friend Brother Ramon telling me that he had been diagnosed with cancer and his condition was serious, my first response was one of personal anguish. I felt a muddled mixture of feelings that included hurt, anger, grief and fear. There was a time when I might have tried to bypass these emotions, somehow feeling that they were not terribly Christian. Surely, I would have thought, the appropriate Christian response is to demonstrate miracle-working faith right at the outset of this? Feelings of fear and anger should be rebuked. I know this response will seem immature and silly to some, but it was borne out of a genuine desire to be true to the fact that our God is a God who does surprise us with acts of power and grace. I was at home with the angels, but I still had much to learn about the wild beasts.

What I am learning now is that it is quite possible to be at home with both the wild beasts (the maelstrom of feelings that arrive when we meet sickness in a friend) and with the angels (those symbols of heaven that remind us that the Spirit of God breaks into the dark places). As I read the stories in the Gospels where Jesus encounters human sickness and suffering, his is a response that also holds these two reactions in tension.

I find the opening chapter of Mark's Gospel fascinating reading. It is action packed, starting with the preaching of John the Baptist in the desert, going on to the baptism of Jesus, the fasting in the wilderness and the calling of the disciples. Then there is a hectic day which includes the deliverance of a man in the Capernaum synagogue, the healing of Simon's mother-in-law, and healing all the sick of the town at sundown. He rises early while it is still very dark and then returns to the fray encountering a leper whom he heals. So many want to receive Jesus' power that he could no longer go into a town openly, and the chapter ends with him in the country with crowds coming out to him. It is a chapter of intense movement and power. But there is also the rhythm of engagement and withdrawal that is such an essential pattern for Jesus. Those moments of withdrawal were for prayer (v. 35), but also the fully human part of him would have needed rest and refreshment. Maybe in this prayer time he had to take back to his Father all that was going on in him as he faced the adulation of the crowds. Those moments apart were not simply times of spiritual renewal but were times of attending to his humanity.

Lest we should think that he left his humanity behind when he engaged in ministry, we find evidence that his healing ministry was rooted both in his divinity and humanity. I see this in the story of the leper (vv. 40ff.). Clearly the power of God was wonderfully released and the leper was restored to good health. But I find myself asking, 'What was it that motivated Jesus to do this healing?' He knew that it was part of the mandate of the Messiah to heal the sick, and therefore he healed because it was part of his mission to do this. But it seems that in this incident it was not the need to demonstrate that he was the Messiah that prompted the healing, for he told the leper not to tell anyone. But I think there was another motivating factor which was more down to earth. In verse 41, Mark tells us that Jesus was 'moved with pity'. I have always liked the Greek word for this which is *splanknizomai*. The *splanchna* are the bowels, the place where deepest feelings are located. Some versions of Mark's Gospel actually have a different word here – they have *orgistheis*, which means 'filled with rage'. I sometimes wonder how they knew what Jesus felt. Did he, just before performing this miracle, turn to one of the disciples and say, 'By the way, when you come to write up this event, could you note that I am deeply moved.' I think it is most unlikely! I think it is much more likely that the disciples watched Jesus carefully at these moments and they saw his face contorting and perhaps his figure bent with emotion, which some read as compassion and some as anger. Whatever the exact nature of the feeling, we know that as Jesus faced this man who had suffered so terribly with leprosy, he felt the pain of it in his own depths, and it was the compassion in him that caused him to reach out his hand and bring the power of God to bear upon the leper's life such that the sickness was cured. This story tells us so clearly that Jesus was not some impassive miracle worker who rather academically healed the sick because it was what Messiahs had to do. He engaged deeply in the suffering of the people that he ministered to. I am grateful to John Woolmer who has helped me to understand this more clearly. In his book, *Healing and Deliverance*,[3] he draws our attention to the following in Matthew's Gospel:

> When Jesus entered Peter's house, he saw his mother-in-law lying in bed with a fever; he touched her hand, and the fever left her, and she got up and began to serve him. That evening they brought to him many who were possessed by demons; and he

cast out the spirits with a word, and cured all who were sick. This was to fulfil what had been spoken through the prophet Isaiah, 'He took our infirmities and bore our diseases.' (8:14–18)

John Woolmer points out that Matthew here is making a link between Jesus' healing ministry and Isaiah 53. For other New Testament writers, Isaiah 53 is the classic prophecy about the atonement, and because they focus exclusively on this aspect, they miss the fact that the prophecy also relates to other parts of Jesus' ministry, in particular his healing ministry. Matthew links Jesus' healing ministry with the work of the Suffering Servant in Isaiah 53. John Woolmer quotes Michael Green who writes,

> But here the Isaiah passage seems to be used with a secondary application. It is related not to the death of Jesus, but to his healing ministry. And it seems to say that so costly was this healing that Jesus took up our infirmities on himself, and carried our diseases. He bore our sickness as well as our sin. There is no suggestion of Calvary here. There is no justification for those who would claim that Jesus bore our sicknesses as well as our sins upon the Cross. But Matthew does see the healing ministry of Jesus as part of the pain and hardship that Isaiah foresaw for the Servant of the Lord in Chapters 40–55 of his book.[4]

Michael Green does acknowledge that sickness is related (though not directly related) to sin, so it is not possible to dissociate the healing ministry from the vicarious ministry of the Cross. But the point he makes is interesting. This connection in Matthew of Jesus' ministry of healing and deliverance with the work of the Suffering Servant certainly seems to suggest that Jesus' encounter with those who were sick was a 'suffering encounter'. He felt the pain of the sickness in his own *splanchna*, guts. His very humanity, perfect though it was, did, in some mysterious way, bear the pain of the very sickness he was healing. There were many other ancillary sufferings as well, to do with the misunderstanding of the crowds, the rejection of the Pharisees, the puzzlement of the disciples, and Mark even hints that his family thought he was out of his mind (Mark 3:21).

This tells us that there is a very costly side to the healing ministry. The healing ministry, if it is to follow the pattern of our Master, is not about us moving in from a place of strength and distributing mighty healing power. It is about us being filled with compassion, and to some extent sharing in the suffering of the person who is seeking healing. In this way the healing ministry makes us very vulnerable. I think this is what makes the telly-evangelist style of ministry so offensive to many of us. The smart-suited evangelist strutting across a stage performing acts of healing to the applause of a big crowd is pandering much more to the needs of people to have strong celebrity figures who are superheroes that have somehow broken free from the normal struggles of life that assail the rest of us. When these champions fall to the 'sins of the flesh', the followers are totally devastated because they had believed that these heroes had elevated themselves above the normal weaknesses of our humanity. Their strength is seen to be in a kind of super-spirituality. But in the ministry of our Lord Jesus, however, we do not see a super-spirituality but rather a wonderful integration of humanity and spirituality, and his healing ministry flows from this integration.

Healing and suffering

Anyone who seeks to engage in the ministry of healing will need a heart open to compassion. The word 'compassion' means literally 'suffering with', and this theme of suffering is very much part of the healing journey. Jesus healed in response to seeing people suffering, and he taught his disciples to do the same. It is this suffering element that causes some people to recoil from the ministry of healing. For a start, to pray for healing with the laying on of hands, for example, means that I have to get close to someone who is sick. I am drawing close to their world. I will need to listen to their pain, and in acute cases that might be unbearable. But there is also the problem of what to do if God does not cure the person. The prayer of healing inevitably raises expectation that a cure is possible, and when that cure does not come then there is the added pain of disappointment. We shall look at this puzzle more closely later in the book.

There is no doubt that when we see people sick or hurting we want them freed of that distress. The fact that God does come with healing grace and power as he did with the leper in Mark 1, has done with countless people down the ages, and continues to do so today, opens us to the hope that he will do it again. But though we long for that complete cure, we will have to be careful not to let our desire for a cure get in the way of a healing work that might not include a cure. Our longings for cures can mean that we fail to listen to the suffering story. We are people of the resurrection and the cross, which means that we will have to be at ease both with the dazzling presence of the risen Lord and also with the suffering servant of the Cross.

The problem with being too cure-focused is that we can become impatient with pain and suffering. Samuel Solivan is Professor of Christian Theology at Newton Theological School in Massachusetts and is an adjunct Professor at the Harvard School of Medicine, Mind, Body Institute. He has written a paper for the *Journal of Pentecostal Theology* called 'The Spirit, Pathos and Liberation'.[5] His work with the Hispanic poor has caused him to invent a new word which he feels we need to take note of. He argues that alongside 'orthodoxy' (correct belief) and 'orthopraxis' (correct ethics and practice) we need 'orthopathos'. He writes:

> Orthopathos is an attempt to bridge the gulf between orthodoxy and orthopraxis ... Pathos points to and highlights the importance that should be given to a people's suffering, dehumanization, pain and marginalization. Orthopathos seeks to show how correct doctrine uninformed by a people's suffering, often tends to be stoic, apathetic and distant.[6]

Perhaps our understanding of the healing ministry needs some 'orthopathos'. Certainly our hope is that the ministry of healing will produce relief from pain and sickness, and naturally we want this to happen as easily and quickly as possible, for no one enjoys pain. But at the same time we need to be very open to learning from the sick and the suffering, for it may well be that they are the ones who are to minister to us. I am just as likely to be changed by being in the presence of someone who is suffering than they are by my prayer for healing. This has come back to me more and more as I reflect on my friends who have been sick. In the case of Brother Ramon, I now see so clearly that we are both on a healing journey. He is the one who is sick with cancer and I pray regularly for his healing. But I have become involved in his journey of healing and I know that I too am being healed of something within me, something that is less obvious, something that I cannot yet put a name to. I think it resides in my soul, and perhaps before I finish this book I will know what it is. At the present time, all I know is that I don't *need* to know! The point is that, by drawing close to someone who is suffering, I have embarked on a healing journey not only in the life of that friend, but also in myself.

The resurrection of the body

Before we leave this chapter on our humanity, one final word about the body. And this is to do with its eternal future. William Temple described the Christian faith as the most materialistic of all the religions. The thought is shocking to some: surely, we follow Christ precisely to *get away from* this materialistic world that so bogs us down. But then we have to consider that ours is a faith that has as its Messiah one who came as flesh and blood, and who lived for thirty years or so as a human being on this earth, and has asked us to remember him in the very physical substances of bread and wine. As we have seen, in the course of that time he became fully aware of what it meant to be human. He modelled for us a life that expressed itself fully in all that makes up our humanity, including the realms of physicality, emotions and spirit.

Well, some may say, then maybe he was labouring under the burden of his humanness while he was in this earthly life, but once he had died, he rid himself of the body once and for all. But, of course, we discover that it is not as simple as that. At the end of his life, we do indeed see a separation of his spirit from his body. On the Cross he offers his spirit to his Father who is spirit (John 4:24: 'God is spirit, and those who worship him must worship in spirit and truth'), and he entrusts his body to Joseph and Nicodemus, who place it in the tomb (John 19:38f.). Come the triumphant resurrection on Easter morning, we might have expected to find a risen Jesus who was totally spiritual. Gone would be the rigours and testing of mortal flesh, and instead would be a completely spiritual, non-material being who had once and for all destroyed the human body. But no; we find something much more mysterious. We find Jesus in a *resurrected body*, and this is puzzling in the extreme. When the disciples first encounter the risen Jesus, they assume he is a ghost. But Jesus replies: 'Look at my hands and my feet; see that it is I myself. Touch me and see; for a ghost does not have flesh and bones as you see that I have' (Luke 24:39). The surprising truth is that when Jesus emerged from the tomb that first Easter morning, he brought his human body with him. The sad fact is that for most of the life of the

Church, Christians have gone into the doors of their churches to worship the risen Lord, doing their best to leave their bodies behind. David Runcorn in his *Rumours of Life*, a book on the resurrection appearances of Jesus, laments this hostility to our bodies, and writes of how in the church the really spiritual parts of our lives are seen to be the most significant, as people have such a negative view of their bodies: 'Our bodies have to come along as well, of course; but like resentful children, dragged by the ears and knowing instinctively where they are not really welcome, they get bored, fidget and cause a distraction. The body is a temporal nuisance.'[7]

The fact that Jesus emerged from the tomb with a resurrection *body* is a challenge to those who constantly attempt to dematerialise the Christian faith. The resurrection body of Jesus certainly had a wonderful spiritual nature which was entirely unhindered by the normal restraints of humanity. It could pass unhindered through locked doors, and it could transport itself wherever it wanted. But it also walked on roads, ate fish, filled its lungs with air to breathe upon the disciples, and invited Thomas to touch the wounds, still evident on the body. It was a body that looked like the Jesus the disciples had known and loved, and even carried on it the marks of his suffering. It is deeply significant that there was a physicality about the resurrection body of Jesus.

Paul expands on this for us in 1 Corinthians 15 where he discusses our future hope which is based on the resurrection of Jesus from the dead. I have always found myself standing back in amazement at this chapter, and very much doubt whether I have begun to grasp the meaning and implications of it. I have read through verses 35ff. again and again trying to take in the truth of this into a deeper place of my soul, because it seems to me that this extraordinary juxtaposition of life now/life hereafter and body/spirit is a key to how to live humanly now and in the afterlife.

To help me understand this passage I have imagined Paul having a conversation with someone – I will imagine it is Silas, and I imagine them sitting under the shade of an apple tree during a rest stop on one of their missionary journeys:

SILAS: Paul, it's all very well going on about a resurrection. But what do you mean by it? What is actually going to happen when I drop dead and I'm just a lump of flesh and blood lying in the earth?

PAUL: Now Silas, don't be such a fool – it's obvious, isn't it?

SILAS (*under his breath*): Perhaps to you, O mighty theologian . . .

PAUL (*ignoring the murmuring*): What have you got in your hand there?

SILAS: A nice Granny Philo apple.

PAUL: OK, take out one of the pips.

SILAS (*munching through to the core*): Yup, here it is.

PAUL: This is the obvious bit. If you want to grow an apple, you don't plant the whole apple, and you certainly don't bury the apply tree under the ground. You get this little seed, and you put it in the ground. And what happens?

SILAS: The seed grows up into a new apple tree.

PAUL: Exactly – so look – compare this little pip, and this wonderful apple tree that we are shading under. One is tiny and rather vulnerable, the other is grand, so big it shelters us from the hot sun, and is full of fruit. So it is with us. Your body now is like that seed. As seeds go it's not bad.

SILAS: Thanks for nothing.

PAUL: But one day it will need to be put in the ground. Now you know as well as I that you are not going to get another Silas growing out of the ground. The old seed rots in the ground. But by the work of the Spirit that raised Jesus from the dead, that seed is transformed in the dark soil of death, and something far more wonderful emerges. Something that will last forever because it also has a spiritual dimension.

SILAS: Mmm. Yes, OK, I understand that bit. But what's this stuff about a 'spiritual body'?

PAUL: Well, think about the two Adams.

SILAS: I can think of one – Adam in the Garden of Eden. Can't think of the other, unless you mean the butcher's lad. He's called Adam, I think.

PAUL: You can't have been awake in the synagogue yesterday. Don't you remember – I was saying that Jesus was like the second Adam.

SILAS (*not convincingly*): Oh, yea, I remember . . .

PAUL: Now think of the first Adam – he was flesh and blood. To be precise, he was formed by the Lord God from the dust of the earth. He was spirit-less, until the Lord God breathed into his nostrils the breath of life, and lo and behold, Adam was fully alive – body and spirit. So the physical came first, and then the spiritual. Now the second Adam, Jesus, was different.

He came from heaven. Adam 1 was from the earth, whereas Adam 2 was from heaven. Now you are a descendant of Adam, and you are a living human – not always obvious, I know – but you are, and you have life here on earth. But what about after death? Well, you are also a relative of Jesus – you are in Christ by faith. So as a relative of him, you also will have life in heaven, after death. And he has shown the way – lots of people we have spoken to saw him after he rose from the dead. We will have a body like that. I call it a 'spiritual body'.

SILAS: So it'll be quite different from this.

PAUL: As different as the seed is from the apple tree. But don't forget, it is related.

SILAS: You know something, Paul, I rather like the thought of seeing you as a spiritual body.

PAUL: Enough of your cheek, Silas. Come on, we've got to catch that boat to Samothrace.

SILAS (*aware of his tired legs*): I wouldn't mind a touch of that resurrection body now . . .

What I find fascinating is the 'body' bit of this. It is clear that in the resurrection life in which we are invited to partake after death, there will be a bodily element. This has implications for us here on earth, because it means there is something about the physical part of our humanity here and now that is so valuable that it will have a part, albeit in a transformed way, in the full perfection of heaven. This means it must have a role in my Christian life now. The most remarkable miracle in all of this is that recorded for us in the book of Revelation.

Then I saw a new heaven and a new earth; for the first heaven and the first earth had passed away, and the sea was no more. And I saw the holy city, the new Jerusalem coming down out of heaven from God, prepared as a bride adorned for her husband. And I heard a loud voice from the throne saying, 'See the home of God is among mortals. He will dwell with them; they will be his peoples, and God himself will be with them.' (Rev. 21:1–3)

This is wonderful and extraordinary. Both heaven *and* earth are to be recreated, not just heaven. There is to be a new physical earth which is to be so perfect that God himself will actually want to live here with humans for eternity. The final vision in Revelation is not a vision of heaven, but a vision of God on earth among a human community. As with all Christian future hope, the vision of the future is given to inspire us in the present. It tells us that, though spoilt, our world and our humanity are treasured by God. They will one day be transformed by him, but thanks to the work of the Holy Spirit, a little of what belongs in the future is available to us now.

A glance at our future hope, therefore, affirms what we have been exploring in this chapter: that our Christian faith is not about trying to escape from the flesh and blood part of our humanity. It is about openly acknowledging its existence, respecting its strengths, and being honest about its weaknesses.

The man who thought he was strong

The man who thought he was strong felt the strength of the motorbike power along the dusty road. He liked the roar of the engine, and the looks of admiration on the faces of the children as they drove through villages.

When they reached the village where the blind girl lived, the man got off the bike and his legs felt bruised and tired. He walked stiffly to a hut as the sun fell behind a tall palm and splinters of light danced with him on the warm sand. The man who thought he was strong saw some people who looked weak and he was glad he had come. He remembered his wealth. He remembered his brother. His legs felt tired, but he knew he was strong.

A child took his hand and talked to him in a language he knew not. A tall man came and smiled, and the man who knew he was strong reached into his shirt and pulled out a picture – the picture of the girl from the village who was blind and poor and needed help. The tall man held the picture and looked at it for a long time.

'You have come to meet Efah,' said the tall man in English.

'I have,' said the man who thought he was strong.

The tall man smiled and invited him into his simple home. As darkness fell, he and his wife gave the man a meal of chicken and maize and told him about their world. They told him that they were a village of three hundred people and they lived in peace. They told him that the girl was the daughter of a good friend, and that she went to the school and could even speak some English. They told him that some in the village spoke English because they felt sorry for the English. The man who thought he was strong laughed at this, but noticed that only he laughed and he heard his laughter drift through the open window. He felt it hurt the dark air outside and he felt ashamed.

They told him about their religion. A poor man came to their village. He was a good man who wore a brown robe. No one spoke his language, but he slowly learned theirs. He lived with them for three years before he spoke about his religion. During that time he listened to them. They then asked him to teach them. He did not have long to teach them for he became ill, but before he died he told them about Paska, a god who was gentle. The man who thought he was strong found it hard to understand their religion. It was so different from his so he started to tell them about his, and his friends listened and smiled.

They invited the man who thought he was strong to stay in their home. He ate and he drank, and in the morning he awoke with a fever. He was afraid. He wanted a phone, a doctor, some medicine. But the woman sang to him and children came and soothed his head with water and someone came and gave him *sips of a sweet liquid. For many days his stomach hurt and his head felt dizzy, and as he sat on an old oil can outside the hut and watched the chickens scratch in the dusty road, the man knew that he was not strong, and he thanked God for these new friends who had cared for him.*

After seven days, the man who knew he was no longer strong, was taken to meet the little girl, the girl in the photo, the girl who was blind, the girl he could help, the girl whose name was Efah.

"AND HOW MUCH MORE VALUABLE YOU ARE!"
Luke 12:24

Chapter 3

The Value of the Sick

As I write this chapter, I am conscious that I write as one who has been in good health for a long time. Apart from a bit of asthma, eczema and backache, I enjoy good health and have hardly ever taken time off sick in my working life. It is therefore very difficult for me to imagine what it must be like to be sick. However, I have been close to a number of good friends who have been seriously sick. One thing I have seen in some of my friends who have been afflicted with cancer is a sense of loss of value, because, like me, up until their sickness they were active and productive in their work and leisure life, and had not known much ill health. I remember visiting one close friend, Paul, when I heard he had been diagnosed with lung cancer. Paul and his family had been very good to me and my wife when we first moved to Kidderminster in the early 1980s. It was my first experience of being a vicar, and I was inevitably rather naive and a bit self-conscious. During these days I made friends with Paul and the thing I appreciated about him was that he could not care less that I was the vicar, he just seemed to like me because I was me. He was a neighbour a few doors down the road from us, and at the time he did not come to church.

When our first child arrived, Paul and his wife Marilyn and their children were a huge support to us, and we developed a deep friendship. In time Paul discovered Christ and faithfully followed him, as did all the family. In a gentle way, Paul was always busy, but he rather enjoyed being a bit behind on schedule, I think, to show that he was not going to be driven by the demands and deadlines of others. In that way, he taught me a lot. Paul was only in his mid fifties when cancer struck him, suddenly and without any warning. When we heard the shocking news, we went to visit him. Typical of Paul, he talked openly and honestly about his life and also the grim prognosis of death in the coming months. As it turned out, only a few weeks later Paul died, more suddenly than anyone expected.

As I reflect on that rather cold November afternoon in Paul and Marilyn's living-room, the scene I remember very clearly is that of Paul going to fetch in some logs from a wheelbarrow outside. It was a normal duty that he had done hundreds of times before in winters gone by. But now the doing of it demanded immense effort. I watched his weakened body struggling with a couple of logs, and the wheezing in his chest betrayed the deadly disease within. This somehow illustrated part of the wretchedness of this illness. Paul, who had been so active, so alive, so hardworking, was now struggling to shift a couple of small logs. He had not been able to go to work for weeks, and his work in the home had been greatly reduced. His life had become focused around the management of this disease that was daily sapping energy from him.

As I thought about this later I realised that if I were in

Paul's situation, the inability to achieve all that I used to achieve would be so hard. I know that says much about my own inadequacies, but I don't think I am that unusual. For someone who has been strong, productive and healthy, the presence of sickness is a most un-welcome intruder that threatens our sense of value. We do live in a society where we are valued according to what we do, rather than who we are. Of course, in Paul's case, none of us considered him of less value because he could no longer do the usual chores around the house. Quite the reverse. In his extreme illness, he became of even greater value, and we all realised just how much we cherished him. But none the less, deep in the psyche of the Western Protestant work ethic, there is the feeling that value is related to productivity.

We are a society that admires those who burn the candles at both ends. Talk to any clergy. Most will freely tell you that they are working at least sixty-hour weeks – and they usually are. I have not yet met a clergy person who has proudly told me that he or she only works thirty hours a week. A madness has come upon us, and the church is as insane as any other part of society. I am told that in Britain, those in work work longer hours than in any other European country. As a result a high percentage of those who have work experience stress and many develop stress-related illnesses.

With this prevailing atmosphere, it is even harder to be non-productive. For many of us, if we are not busily engaged in relentlessly pursuing targets and reaching deadlines, both in our place of work and our home, we start to get worried. It doesn't feel right, something must be wrong. I count myself among those who are sick with this disease, and I know it is due to choices I have made, but it is also due to the society I live in, where this particular sickness is so infectious. But in the midst of this sick society are some apparently sick people who may actually have a health that many of us do not have.

To be or not to be

Almost twenty years ago I wrote the Grove booklet, *The Wisdom to Listen*.[1] I wrote it just as I was embarking on the Anglican ministry into which I was ordained. I did not have much wisdom at that stage in my life, but I had learned the value of listening, and it does not altogether surprise me that I now work for the Acorn Christian Foundation heading up Christian Listeners.[2] One thing that has remained firmly within me throughout my ministry is the importance of this ministry of listening. In the booklet I wrote a section on hyperactivity in which I lamented the high speed, high pressure nature of the world we live in, which inevitably makes us less able to listen to ourselves, to one another and to God. In the last twenty years, there have been signs that in the Christian Church people are increasingly longing for space and peace, and the growth of the retreat movement is a sign of this. But by and large, life, for many of us, still goes at a breathless pace, and that lack of breath is endangering our souls.

Whilst I continue to be concerned about the pressures we put ourselves under in all of this, increasingly I worry about those who are not part of the busy brigade. I worry about how we treat those like my friend Paul, whose sickness has meant that they have had to become 'unproductive'; those with disabilities, many of whom have to move slowly because of their disability; the unemployed who feel very left behind as they see the employed speeding down motorways to lucrative business deals. Although many of us don't like our busyness, we like the sense of significance it gives us. Clergy would not want to say, 'I only work thirty hours a week', because they know that their fellow clergy, their parish and society generally would regard them as ineffective and lazy. I suspect they would be deeply resented. Our value is defined by our productivity and industriousness. It is a bitter fruit of our industrialised society.

If we take a look at the Gospels we see something rather different. Granted, the Gospels are about events in a society in the first century that did not have the burdens of the information superhighway. However, the Roman Empire was definitely one that was very conscious of productivity and achievement. Into this society comes the Messiah, who proclaims a gospel of grace which is demonstrated right at the outset of his ministry. At his baptism in the river Jordan, the voice of his Father in heaven proclaims that Jesus is his beloved Son in whom he delights. The word of affirmation is given to Jesus before he has begun the work of the Kingdom. The approval is for who he is, not for what he has achieved.

The starting point of value is therefore in being, not in doing. Jesus showed in his own life that the productivity of people was neither here nor there when it came to value. Certainly the least valued of that society, the children, the women and the poor, were given great value by Jesus. He also valued the sick. There are many

Gospel stories about his encounters with the sick. But was he only interested in them because he was about to heal them? Were they only of value because they would be useful in the Kingdom cause of demonstrating that God could do powerful things such as healings? I have seen some healings in church meetings which convey exactly this – that sick people are 'useful' as a means of demonstrating that the healer is powerful. However, in the healing ministry of our Lord Jesus, I see something very different. The love and compassion that he shows to the suffering is there irrespective of their healing.

Take, for example, Mark's story of the healing of the deaf man:

> They brought to him a deaf man who had an impediment in his speech; and they begged him to lay his hand on him. He took him aside in private, away from the crowd, and put his fingers into his ears, and he spat and touched his tongue. Then looking up to heaven, he sighed and said to him, 'Ephphatha', that is, 'Be opened.' And immediately his ears were opened, his tongue was released, and he spoke plainly. Then Jesus ordered them to tell no one; but the more he ordered them, the more zealously they proclaimed it. (Mark 7:32–6)

If Jesus was only interested in this man for the purposes of healing he would have shown no consideration to him as a deaf person. However, we see him showing great sensitivity to the man in his condition of deafness. He takes him away from the crowds; he touches his ears and his tongue communicating to the man in a language he understands that he is intending to help him with those two areas of his body which are so far uncured; he looks to heaven indicating that he is praying; he says the word '*Ephphatha*', a word easy to lip-read. The man would have felt greatly valued and respected in his deafness by these considerate actions of Jesus. The man is cured, but Jesus instructs him not to tell anyone, which is another indication that he is not doing this healing to impress the crowds. As it happens, the man who is healed of dumbness just cannot but tell the whole world what has happened to him! In his deafness and dumbness the man would have felt of little value in the culture of first-century Palestine. But in those few moments before his cure, he felt supremely valued. No doubt this was as vital a part of the healing as the removal of the deafness and dumbness.

It is sad that Christians can all too easily be caught up in the general mindset of the intolerance of imperfections, uselessness and losing. A church which has engaged in a ministry of healing can be quick to make judgements on people who have sicknesses or disabilities. We have already considered the extreme end of this, where those who are sick or disabled can be made to feel doubly bad about themselves at healing meetings, where they are accused of having insufficient faith or harbouring unconfessed sins. But thankfully, there are others who are countering this cruel approach and who have much to teach us. One such person is Jean Vanier, founder of L'Arche Community.

L'Arche

In the 1950s a young man called Jean Vanier left the Navy to live in a small Christian community founded by a Dominican priest with the purpose of studying philosophy and theology, and to live the gospel values of prayer and welcoming the poor. He was a Doctor of Philosophy. In his life in the community he came into contact with an institution of thirty men with mental handicaps.[3] These men profoundly affected him, and he gave up lecturing philosophy, and he began visiting institutions and mental hospitals. In August 1964, he welcomed two men from the institution into his own home – Raphael and Philippe. These three lived in a small, rather broken-down house in Trosly-Breuil in Northern France. The story of L'Arche had begun. The community has become a network of over a hundred small communities in many different countries. In each community there live men and women with a range of intellectual abilities and disabilities. They lead lives of simplicity and mutual support. In his book, significantly entitled *Becoming Human*, Jean Vanier writes,

> Strangely enough, this process of becoming human occurred most profoundly for me when I started living with men and women with intellectual disabilities, people who are not very capable on the intellectual or practical level, but who are very gifted in relationships. They are people of the heart, people of trust. With them I began to discover that human maturity comes as we begin to bring our heads and our hearts together. In my early adulthood, I had developed my intellectual and rational capacities; living with people who had disabilities called me to develop my capacity to relate to others. With them I

learned how to become more open and vulnerable to others, especially to those who are different.[4]

In a world in which people are finding it increasingly difficult to know how to relate to others, Jean Vanier's message is becoming vitally important.

I am writing this just after returning from our summer holiday which we spent on a campsite in South Brittany. In the evenings my family and I would wander up to the bar, and always at the heart of this thriving throbbing place was a lively group of teenagers, breaking loose from the shackles of school and family life, and fully equipped with designer clothes and hair gels they made the most of the social scene. My wife and I were not alone as parents rather anxiously watching their teenage children drawn into this whirlpool of adolescent adventure! One evening there was a karaoke, and I remember going to the bar to fetch our drinks, and hearing a rather torturous version of Chris de Burgh's 'Lady in Red' being sung. Grasping my cool Pastis, I wandered over to the dance floor to see who was singing and I discovered that the singer was part of a small group of people with intellectual disabilities who were holidaying at the campsite. He was Frederick, singing with heart and soul, and behind him on a giant screen was a film of the stereotypical handsome able man, dancing with the stereotypical beautiful blonde. All kinds of emotions piled into me as I watched Frederick singing with such fullness – shame at my original judgement of the singing; wonder at the sheer beauty of his heart; sorrow at my world that could only portray beauty in stereotypical ways, and cause many of those young people to be anxious about their appearance and afraid to be themselves. I could sense that Frederick had discovered beauty in a way that they and I had yet to know it.

The following night I found myself sitting next to Frederick. Immediately he turned to me and spoke to me in fluent French. I understood very little, but with the little French I had, and screaming over the sound of the disco, we managed a kind of conversation and I discovered that he and his friends were part of a L'Arche community. My lack of French made no difference to him, and for a time he nattered on in French, and I responded as best I could, knowing that in these few moments there was a communion of hearts that did not really need language. Most of the communicating involved broad smiles and nods of the head. Frederick was teaching me about relationships. I was not very good at learning, and I realised how disabled I was. But I think I was healed a little bit that evening, though not fully cured by any means.

Many have found L'Arche to be an inspirational and prophetic witness. In November 1995 a group of theologians gathered to reflect on the implications of the values and lifestyle of L'Arche. All those who gathered one way or another had their lives touched by disability, and had cause to be grateful to the work of L'Arche. The reflections of this group have been published in a book entitled *Encounter with Mystery*, and is edited by Frances Young.[5] One contributor to this work is John Goldingay. At the time of writing, John is a Professor of Old Testament Studies at Fuller Theological Seminary in Pasadena. But before this, he was Principal of St John's College, Nottingham. John was on the staff at

St John's when I was a student there in the late 1970s. There was an endearing wildness about John, always lively and full of energy and humour. Old Testament lectures were seldom boring when he was teaching. John is married to Ann, and while I was at college, Ann was suffering from multiple sclerosis. I did not get to know John and Ann very well, but I was most impressed by the balance they achieved in their lives – John so energetic, and Ann forced to live a stiller life by her illness. It did not surprise me to see that John was a contributor to *Encounter with Mystery*, offering his reflections as husband and theologian on Ann's illness. His chapter is entitled 'Being Human'.

In his chapter, John Goldingay explores what it means for humanity to be made in God's image, and suggests that people who are disabled have the capacity to reveal aspects of humanity which have been suppressed, especially in the modern culture. He argues that all communities need the gifts of those with disabilities, and that 'communities without disabled people are disabled communities'. He writes that disabled people,

> ... have the capacity to reveal to humanity a facet of being human from which the abled can often hide – that is our weakness, vulnerability, and dependence...They embody the fact that there is sometimes a mysterious power in poverty, vulnerability and weakness – a power to move and transform.[6]

Another contributor to this book is David Ford, the Regius Professor of Divinity at Cambridge University. He takes up the theme of disability in his *The Shape of*

Living (the Archbishop of Canterbury's Lent Book for 1998) and writes about the influence of L'Arche on his thinking and feeling. As with John Goldingay, David Ford encourages us to learn from those who have disabilities. One such gift is touch:

> Touching is even more basic. It flows through the day – dressing, eating, carrying, hair care, bathing, playing and just literally keeping in touch. Above all, what struck me was its gentleness. The violence of our times is horrendous – physical violence, institutional violence, spiritual violence. It is intensified by being vividly presented in the media, so that violence often dominates imaginations as well as behaviour. Yet, here at L'Arche was a practice of touching, of handling people, which seemed like a prophetic sign of an alternative. It had enabled gentleness to be at the heart of this community.[7]

In an age which is so confused about touch, these communities have much to teach us indeed.

What is emerging therefore is the need, in the ministry of healing, to view those with disability and the 'uncured' with the greatest respect, and with the expectation that there is likely to be a two-way healing flow. I first became aware of this when I visited India early in 1996. I was part of a team invited by the Bishop of East Kerala, and the focus of the mission was evangelism and healing. The mission took place under a large awning by the cathedral which stood on the hillside overlooking the tropical forest and a plain that stretched out to the misty coast and the Indian Ocean. Next to the cathedral was a school that catered for children who had been afflicted with polio, that disease that is known as the scourge of India. The mission was a week long and there were meetings during the day and in the evenings.

One day, after the morning meeting, the Bishop said to me, 'Michael, I would like you to speak on healing at this evening's meeting and then lead in the healing ministry.' Thankfully, I had the afternoon to prepare, and I was given a room in the polio school. On the way down the hill to the school I felt God prompting me to speak on the healing of the lame man by Peter and John at the Beautiful Gate in Jerusalem as recorded in Acts 3. So, when I arrived in my simple room in the school building, I reached for my Bible and notebook and started scribbling down some thoughts. The warm Indian air filled the room and confidence arose as I set about writing the talk. But there was one distraction: one of the windows in the room I had been given looked out onto a corridor, down which passed many of the students of the school. Once it was known that the English priest was writing his sermon in this room, it was necessary for every member of the school to come and have a look. Thus there began a procession of fascinated faces at the window along with knocks on the glass and a good deal of laughter. Generally speaking it was fatal for me to show I had noticed as this precipitated much more interest, but I could not help but notice on one occasion one small boy pulling himself up to peer in through the window. He had no use in his legs, and it took him all his effort to pull his broken body up and peer at the English sermon-writing phenomenon. Suddenly I felt a sense of horror: here I was writing a sermon on the healing of a lame man, and right next to me, in fact surrounding me, engulfing me, was a large number of children, all of whom had a disease which was disabling.

My horror was a sense of hypocrisy. Here I was using my theological gifts to craft a sermon on the healing of the lame man, and yet I was quite incapable of helping this lame child. I felt terribly fraudulent, and I prayed that God would change me to make me the kind of person that he could use in the healing ministry. I thought of all those telly-evangelist types whose styles of ministry I hated, but who seem to get results of healing. I asked God to make me even like them if it would mean that one of these little ones could walk freely. As I grew more and more confused and distressed, I heard a still small voice which seemed to say, 'But who is the most sick here?' To me, it was obvious – they could not walk, and I could. But the question went on, 'Who is the most sick? Can you smile like they smile?' I noticed the smiles on the faces of these children – smiles that seemed to be so open, so good, so gracious and uncomplaining in their suffering. And I thought of my smile – I felt my smile. It felt a tired smile by comparison. But worse than that, it did not feel like a proper smile, because it was an infected smile. Gradually I became aware of a disease within me. It is difficult to give a name to this disease, but I knew it was related to my Western-ness. It was to do with my wealth, and the wealth of my nation. It was to do with the consumerism of my Western culture, and the way it had soured my soul. It was to do with the materialism that made it so hard for me to appreciate simplicity. In those moments I became terribly and painfully aware of the corruption and sickness in my soul, and I acknowledged that I too was sick, and that I could not emotionally and spiritually walk freely as my friends the other side of that window could.

That evening I did preach on the healing of the lame man by the Gate Beautiful, and after I preached I went down the row of children whose limbs were twisted and deformed, but whose hearts were far more able than mine. And I did pray for them to be healed, because I still longed that they might walk and run freely. But I also asked God to heal me through them, and I do believe that night something deep within me was touched. I think I am only partially healed, but I know something within me has never been the same since then.

Heal the sick

At this point I can hear someone saying, 'So do we not bother to pray for healing any more? Do we go to all sick people and say, "I'm sicker than you, we're all in it together – tough!"' One thing I have learned in this healing ministry is that there are many mysteries. If I read the Gospels, there is no doubt that Jesus commands his disciples to go out to preach the good news, heal the sick and deliver the demonised. I see no reason why we should stop doing this, and personally I will pray for the sick for the rest of my life because my reading of the Gospels, and my understanding of the Church's witness through history, is that this is one of the ways we share the love of God in a broken world. The issue is not so much whether we should engage in the ministry of healing the sick, but *how* do we do it? What I am learning is that what is required is a fundamental mixture of faith and humility. Faith is the childlike knowledge that our God is a mysterious and very loving God who sometimes chooses to defy our rationalism and visit us with remarkable acts of power and grace such that sick people are cured. Humility acknowledges that healing is not about a powerful well person doing healing to a powerless sick person. It respects the person who is sick or disabled and will only pray for healing if that person genuinely desires it; it also acknowledges that that person may have gifts of health that I do not have, and that any healing encounter will involve me being open to receiving healing too. It is a more vulnerable way, and possibly a more painful way. But I think it is the way of the Kingdom of God.

Story part 3:

The man who thought he was well

The man who thought he was well was taken to the girl who was blind, the girl whom he had read about, the girl whom he had come to help, the girl whose name was Efah.

'You are the man who is not well,' said Efah, sitting on a three-legged stool, and stroking the head of a mongrel dog who lay at her feet.

'No,' said the man who knew he was well, 'I had a fever for a few days, but I'm fine now', and he heard his words which sounded too loud in the hut, and he shuffled his foot and bit his lower lip. He looked at Efah who, with her sightless eyes, was staring at ill-fitting slats of wood that hung as shutters over the gap in the wall that was the window. He felt the silence of the room, a dark room with little furniture and a dusty floor, and sunlight blazing outside, casting bright shafts of light through the shutters. He felt the nervousness rise up in him, a nervousness that needed words to stop the silence.

'I saw your picture – on the net, I mean my computer – at home in England.'

Efah smiled. 'Tell me about computer. Is he a friend?'

'Oh yes, it is a great friend – when it works – just

don't speak to me about Windows,' he chuckled, relieved to feel the smile on his face, but he noticed it did not stay very long and he almost wondered why. Efah did not smile.

'All my friends have windows,' she said, and the man who thought he was well felt perplexed. He wanted to make a joke, but no joke came, only more silence. 'Did you know that Paska is a window?' said Efah into the beckoning silence.

The man who knew he was well said nothing. Efah smiled and now looked with her sightless eyes in the direction of the man who knew he was well, and her dark sightless eyes probed his soul, searching not with curiosity but with something that felt to the man very much like compassion, and he felt discomfort in his chest and heard the noise of his breathing.

'When did you lose your sight?' the man who knew he was well asked the girl who was blind.

'When I was a young child,' she began as a shaft of light that had been moving across the silent room now touched Efah's face, tinging her dark hair with flame, 'I swam in the river, the dark friend who gives us life and carries our boats and gives us food. I swam with my dark friend, but she had been visited by a disease from the city many miles upstream. I felt the pain in my eyes and even though I was young, I knew that these windows were being shut. One of the last things I saw was the man in the dark robe leaning over me and saying words of hope.'

'He asked Paska to heal you?' enquired the man who knew he was well. Efah did not hear his question for she was remembering.

'He died at the same time as my windows were closed and I knew his and my prayer had been answered. We all wept, especially Paska.'

'But you are still blind,' said the man who knew he was well, now irritated with Paska and the man in the brown robe who had given false hope to Efah.

'Is that what you think?' asked Efah, and she turned her face to the man who was well, and the beam of light illuminated her cheeks which were lifted up in a gentle smile, and tears moistened her sightless eyes, and for an awful moment the man who knew he was well realised that the tears were compassion for him. As Efah looked upon him with her sightless eyes, the man felt that he was in one of his dreams where he found he had no clothes on and there was nowhere to hide. In the darkened room with shafts of light, and under the gaze of the sightless eyes he began to see that he could not see.

The man who was beginning to see that he was not well said, 'I would like to talk to you more, Efah,' and Efah said, 'I would like to listen to you more', and for seven days they talked and listened in the darkened room, and trust grew as the sun rose higher and the air grew hotter and the banks of hard-caked mud grew larger on either side of the dark friend.

though I walk through the valley of the
shadow of death -------

Chapter 4

Listening in the Darkness

Although it has taken me a long time to realise it, I am
becoming increasingly convinced that as a Christian I
do not have to know all the answers, neither do I have
to live my Christian life as a great success story. This
can take some believing, especially if you are a Christian
leader. I find that so many Christians of all traditions
have a very low opinion of their Christian lives. I am
often taken aback when I discover that people who are
very successful in their places of work, are often riddled
with insecurities and a sense of inadequacy when it
comes to their Christian faith. It is not surprising therefore that when it comes to healing, many Christians
assume it is the responsibility of those they deem as
experts. They feel far too inadequate to tackle anything
as exalted as healing. As a leader I often feel ashamed
that somehow or other we have managed to convey this
message that only we can do the 'really important'
ministries in the church. Perhaps it is we who are
leaders who have to lead the way in breaking the mould,
and to do this, we will have to acknowledge the wild
beasts within us, and give up the conspiracy that exists
in many churches that we are among the angels!

For eight years I had the privilege of being Director of

Anglican Renewal Ministries. Not long after my appointment, I found to my astonishment that people from all over the country wanted me to speak at big meetings and write erudite books. In some cases I felt very unnerved, because they assumed that, as I had been appointed Director of this national renewal organisation, I must be a very gifted fellow. Any such fantasies were dispelled as soon as I opened my mouth, but none the less I was aware, as any leader is, of a kind of responsibility that is about reassuring others that you are confident in your faith and full of ever burning visions. When clergy would come to our annual conferences I often saw them very worn down by similar expectations from their churches, and one of the things I very much valued about our conferences was that they became safe places for clergy to share their wild beasts of anxieties, fears, frustrations, lusts and longings, and in the doing so opened themselves up to the glorious grace of God. I never ceased to be impressed with the quality of lives that came to those conferences – people who had given themselves so sacrificially to serve others, often for very little thanks.

About halfway through my time with ARM, when it was probably at its most successful, we suddenly hit huge financial problems. When we held our National Conference in the autumn of 1993, we had the task of telling the conference that we were in severe difficulties. People generously responded, but we were not out of trouble, and we had the hideous experience of receiving phone calls every day from creditors chasing us for delayed payments of bills. By November most of us on the staff were not getting any income, and the Trustees launched a last desperate appeal, and took the hard decision to release some of the staff. To fail so publicly felt very humiliating, and to go through the pain of seeing good friends being made redundant was terrible. But in the middle of it all we felt the tender and wounded hands of God steering us through. I think it was during that time that I let go of the need to be a truly-glorious-and-always-wonderfully-successful-and-shiny-Christian. I realised that even in charismatic renewal where the focus is so often on power, it was OK to be vulnerable and power-less. In fact, I was discovering, much of charismatic life was actually about being vulnerable. I do believe that God allowed that experience to help us change the focus of our understanding of the renewal, and I must admit that since that time I have always been a bit anxious about some of the talk about renewal and revival, because it can all too easily convey a bypassing of this vulnerability.

A journey into mysticism

In what turned out to be my last year with ARM I was granted a sabbatical. In the months leading up to this I found I was very weary, and spiritually I felt I was in a very dry wilderness. I felt somewhat fraudulent going around promoting renewal, when in my heart I felt very unrenewed. I remember on one of those horrible November days when everything seems foggy and damp and dark I bumped into part of myself that actually seemed to be doubting everything. I even began to wonder what life would be like without my faith – it was a frightening experience. For the first time I realised that much of what I had in this world depended on me remaining a

Christian. If my faith went, I would lose my job, my community of friends in the church, my income and my house. I had not trained for anything else, so it would mean a long time of redundancy. The materialist in me warned me in no uncertain terms not to pursue this line of thinking! But what actually helped tremendously was a talk I had at that time with the writer and speaker, Adrian Plass. I visited him while I was doing some work in the south of England and we spent some time chatting away in his kitchen. At one point, rather transparently, I said, 'Do you come across people who have lost their faith?' 'Oh yes,' said Adrian calmly (which in itself was rather reassuring) and then added, 'I think a lot of people have to lose their faith so that they can find Jesus again.' Suddenly it felt like a summer beam of sunlight shone through my November fog, and I realised then that the quest for my sabbatical was to rediscover the Jesus that I was in severe danger of losing. I have since decided that it is probably a process that we have to go through more than once in our Christian lives – a kind of shedding of our outer skin of faith, and allowing something new and fresh to appear as we rediscover Jesus.

Wearily, but with a sense of excitement I approached my sabbatical. Two weeks before the sabbatical started, I was hosting an ARM Saturday Conference in Derby with Bishop Graham Dow and a team from the London Diocese. When I got home from the conference, I received the news that my mother had died. For the past six years she had been suffering with Alzheimer's disease, and in many ways it was a relief to know that she was out of the dark valleys of confusion that had besieged her through this terrible illness. None the less our family knew a great sense of loss. My sabbatical therefore began with my conducting the funeral service for my mother. A few days later I was just setting off for a retreat at Glasshampton Monastery when the news came through that a very good friend, Ros Harding, had died very suddenly of a brain tumour at the early age of forty-nine. John and Ros had been a very formative influence on me when I was in my twenties, and we had been close friends since. It was dreadfully shocking to hear of Ros' sudden death, especially as I was still smarting from recent deaths of two other good friends. I therefore arrived at Glasshampton very tired, grieving and aware of my soul's spiritual wilderness. Although I did not realise it then, I had reached the level of vulnerability needed for God to begin to touch and change me.

At Glasshampton I had a long discussion with my hermit friend, Brother Ramon SSF, and he urged me to start reading some of the Christian mystics. The rest is hard to explain, but in his little chapel in the hermit enclosure we had some prayer together and we read a poem by the Victorian poet, Augusta Theodosia Drane, entitled 'What the Soul Desires'. The poem is a beautiful account of someone who is longing to encounter the love of God:

> There is a rapture that my soul desires,
> There is a something that I cannot name;
> I know not after what my soul aspires,
> Nor guess from whence the restless longing came;
> But ever from my childhood have I felt it,
> In all things beautiful and all things gay,

> And ever has its gentle, unseen presence
> Fallen, like a shadow-cloud across my way.

The poem goes on to describe the quest, and then the poet gives an account of how, once, she did discover that for which she was looking:

> Once, only once, there rose the heavy curtain,
> The clouds rolled back, and for too brief a space
> I drank in joy as from a living fountain
> And seemed to gaze upon it, face to face:
> But of that day and hour who shall venture
> With lips untouched by seraph's fire to tell?
> I saw Thee, O my Life! I heard, I touched Thee, –
> Then o'er my soul once more the darkness fell.[1]

In the moments of reading this poem my soul felt more full of light than it had done for a long time. I realised that the busyness of my life had caused so much clutter to gather around my faith that it was hard to find the real thing. I was in the final stages of 'losing my faith' so that I could rediscover Jesus. In these moments I was experiencing in a new way the love of God, and it was a love that shone warm and welcoming on my soul.

For the rest of my three-month sabbatical I read much about the Christian mystical tradition. I discovered that there was actually much common ground between renewal and the mystical tradition. Bishop Morris Maddocks in his book on Dorothy Kerin (the founder of Burrswood) writes:

> Mysticism represents the very heart of religion and the Christian mystic down the ages has contributed

much to the Church's spiritual life, in many instances fanning dying embers into a living flame once more. In fact the Church has been renewed time and again by the fresh and refreshing contacts of its mystics with God. They have been called the eyes of the Body of Christ. Frequently they have supplied that prophetic element in the life of the Church.[2]

Bishop Morris goes on to describe the stages commonly experienced in the mystical tradition, and they are as follows:

(1) *Purgation* – as the name suggests, this is to do with a time of suffering, but it is productive suffering, a suffering that actually leads to something.

(2) *Illumination* – this is the point at which it feels like someone has turned on the light; it is the moment of seeing, of discovery. It is a prophetic moment.

(3) *Union* – this is what Augusta Drane experienced: a moment of being completely taken up in the love of God, a rapture, a visionary experience like that of St Paul as described in 2 Corinthians 12:2ff.:

> I know a person in Christ who fourteen years ago was caught up to the third heaven – whether in the body or out of the body I do not know; God knows. And I know that such a person – whether in the body or out of the body I do not know; God knows – was caught up into Paradise and heard things that are not to be told, that no mortal is permitted to repeat.

Paul's experience clearly followed this pattern. He has

been suffering through this thorn in the flesh (*purgation*), but there then came the experience of being transported to heaven (*illumination*) and seeing wonderful things. Further on in the passage he heard those matchless words, 'My power is made perfect in weakness' and I suspect hearing that was an experience of knowing God very closely and intimately (*union*).

In my own experience I could see the same pattern. The 'purgation' of the bereavements and the spiritual wilderness gave way to that moment of 'illumination' in Brother Ramon's little chapel, and opened the door to tasting a new 'union' with the love of God. I have since seen this simple pattern lived out time and time again in my life and the lives of others. Once again we are being beckoned to a place of owning with honesty what is going on in our humanity. The process of purgation can indeed seem like a devouring wild beast, and yet when faced in the presence of the Rock Dove Spirit, we see it is possible to subdue such wild beasts at the feet of Jesus, and become open to the word of God bringing a new illumination.

Mysticism and healing

The more I have thought about the stage of 'purgation' the more I am convinced that this includes all the difficult experiences of life, ranging from the irritating nitty-gritty of normal everyday life through to the more severe sufferings experienced by those in places of deep pain. Therefore when we bring our wounded friends to receive healing prayer, we will want to be aware that they may well be on a journey that is about discovering a new depth of the love of God. I realise that this can sound all very pious and of little comfort to someone who is suffering. If I am in pain, whether niggling or distressing, everything in me wants rid of it. But no doubt St Paul wanted rid of his thorn in the flesh, and quite likely he took medicines and asked Christian friends to pray for him, before he realised that it was a purgation that was to lead to a new discovery of God's love.

The Victorian poet, Francis Thompson, is well known for his remarkable 'The Hound of Heaven' which has fascinated Christians and non-Christians alike. He was a man who lived a tortured life, and in this poem he writes about how it felt as if God was like a hound chasing him:

> I fled Him, down the nights and down the days;
> I fled Him, down the arches of the years;
> I fled Him, down the labyrinthine ways
> Of my own mind; and in the midst of tears
> I hid from Him, and under running laughter,
>> Up vistaed hopes I sped;
>> And shot, precipitated,
> Adown Titanic glooms of chasmed fears,
> From those strong Feet that followed, followed after.

The poem goes on for several pages, and as you read it you can feel the exhaustion of running, and you feel the relentlessness of the Pursuer. Finally, towards the end of the poem, the running ceases:

> Halts by me that footfall:
> Is my gloom after all
> Shade of His hand, outstretched caressingly?

'Ah, fondest, blindest, weakest,
I am He Whom thou seekest!
Thou dravest love from thee, who dravest Me'.

These lines came to me with new force in those early days of my sabbatical. I had for months assumed that the darkness I had experienced had indicated that I was in a period of the absence of God's presence. But as I read these lines, I realised that my gloom was after all the shade of his hand outstretched caressingly. All along I had assumed that the darkness had meant his absence. But then, and I remember the amazing sense of tenderness as I discovered this, I knew that my 'gloom' was none other than a shadow cast by the caressing hand of God. The very darkness that I had come to despise was in fact his tender touch, and I had been like Francis Thompson, running, running, running with my busy life, failing to stop and allow that caressing hand to touch me. I could have had people praying for my healing and deliverance, but actually what I needed was that moment of illumination. My Christian life has had its ups and downs since then, but that sense of the caressing hand of God has never left me.

Those of us who engage in the healing ministry, then, will have to be careful listeners. I don't think it is ever wrong to pray for healing when asked to, and to cry out to God for our sick friends and family. But in our asking, we will also need to be listening. We will need to listen to our sick friend, and we and they will need to listen to God. This will be risky, because it may well involve us in listening to the wild beasts within us – our fears and dreads, or longings and desperate hopes, and the many confusing emotions that are evoked when someone close to us suffers. But all these are gathered into our healing journey. We will also need to listen to our pain, and this may be the most difficult voice to listen to.

Listening to our pain

In our Western society we see pain as an enemy to be eliminated as quickly and efficiently as possible. Of course, no one in their right mind would choose to endure pain, and the more acute the pain the more desperate we become to eliminate it. But we live in a society where much pain can be eliminated relatively easily. But for most people in the world, painkillers are few and far between.

Some years ago I visited Kenya to take part in a mission just south of Nairobi. Before the start of this mission, I decided to spend the weekend in Northern Kenya with an old friend of mine from college days, Benjamin Muhalya. Ben is an Anglican priest and at the time I visited him, he was vicar of a small town called Eldama Ravine. It was wonderful to meet up with this good friend and to see the churches growing in his parish, to receive his simple and loving hospitality and to take part in the church worship on the Sunday. On the Monday he kindly travelled back to Nairobi with me to keep me company. We travelled in the usual form of public transport, the Matatu. For those who have not travelled in East Africa, I need to explain that a Matatu is something that is a relative of the minibus. You put as many people as possible into it, plus a few more and find a driver who has similar driving ambitions to Michael Schumacher. You are then hurled at high speed along pot-holed roads whilst praying for as many angels as possible to join you on the journey. On this particular journey the pot-holes were impressive and I began to understand what it must be like to be trapped in a tumble dryer. At one point my poor friend Ben knocked his head very hard against the roof and he developed a headache. I felt foolish as I heard myself asking if Ben had an aspirin, as I quickly realised that for Ben and many like him, there was no money for luxuries like aspirins for headaches. He simply had to endure it, and I noticed how he had learned to cope with pain in a way I had not even begun to. Almost every time I get a headache now, I find myself thinking of Ben and it prompts me to pray for him with thanksgiving.

The lack of easily available medicines in the two-thirds world means that pain cannot be removed so easily and efficiently. As a result it has to be listened to more. Some years ago I was in Glastonbury and I decided to look in some of the New Age bookshops to see what books were popular in this movement. I came across one called *Ritual: Power, Healing and Community*, written by a man called Malidoma Patrice Somé. I bought the book and found it a fascinating read. Malidoma comes from the Dagara people of West Africa. Though deeply immersed in his native indigenous culture, he has also chosen to live part of his life in the West. He holds three Masters degrees and two Ph.Ds. He understands well the rationalism and materialism of the West, but he criticises many of the West's values. He has been in demand in the USA especially giving seminars that are to do with teaching the values of his indigenous culture and finding ways of applying them to the materialist West. I found his comments on pain interesting:

> Pain is our body complaining about an intruder. Body complaint is understood as the soul's language relayed to us. A person in pain is being spoken to by that part of themselves that knows only how to communicate in this way ...To shut down the pain, is to override the call of the soul. When this happens it is a repressive measure taken against oneself, which has sombre consequences.[3]

I feel challenged by this. How often I reach for my aspirin, when perhaps the healthier thing is to spend a few moments listening to what my body is trying to tell me. It might be complaining about an intruder, and that intruder may be something that is going on in my life that is not meant to be there. The pain might be the call of my soul. For many people in the West, pain is their body saying 'you are doing too much, you need to rest'. As I write I am aware of the dull backache which has been with me for almost a year and which I have found very frustrating. I can't do things that I used to do. I complain that it makes me feel older than I want to feel. I have arguments with it all the time. I would like it to be healed. But all the time I have a sneaky suspicion that it is trying to say something to me. I acknowledge that I am still rather deaf when it comes to listening to my own body, but perhaps by the time I finish writing this book, I might have heard, and I think when I have heard, then either the pain will ease or I will learn to treat it as a friend.

Beginning with love

The mystical tradition reminds us that all humans long for an encounter with the love of God and as I think about the healing journey, I am aware that love is that which gives us the energy to walk the road. I remember being in one meeting in my local church once where ministry was taking place. It was during the time of the so-called 'Toronto blessing', that rather wonderfully untidy (so good for us Brits) renewal that bubbled up in many churches in the mid 1990s. One of the great things about living in Derby is that the Convent of the Holy Name is based here, and some of the sisters come to our church. On this occasion a couple of sisters brought a young black novice with them who was visiting from Namibia. This novice did not speak a lot of English and she must have wondered what on earth was going on for much of the time. Towards the end of the meeting, people were invited to go forward for ministry – that is to receive prayer for God's blessing for healing, renewal, refreshment and any other help. In the days of this renewal, the ministry offered was rather haphazard, and there was every kind of manifestation imaginable going on.[4] Those of us offering prayer would wander among the crowd of people coming forward and offer to pray for each person. I remember being so impressed that the young Namibian novice came forward straightaway and someone prayed for her. She remained where she was standing, more or less in the midst of the crowd of people who had come forward for the ministry. As she stood there she began to look very vulnerable, and I noticed she leaned her head on one side and brought her thumb up to her mouth. At the time I was engaged in praying for someone else, but I determined to go over to her to check out how she was. However, before I could get to her, one of the English sisters came over to her. This sister then knelt down before her Namibian friend and took her hand, and I sensed a most unusual overflow of love and compassion pouring out from the heart of this sister. I found the scene utterly exquisite: here in the midst of charismatic mayhem, was a scene of beautiful tranquillity. It was like a prophetic witness – that here, in the midst of all the chaos of our woundedness, is an example of the love of Christ. For he too comes through the storms and kneels to wash our feet and restore us.

That little scene has never left me, and it has made me realise that what is needed in the ministry of healing, more than any skills or training, is a humble and loving heart. The one who is to pray for another for healing does not have to be an expert at healing. I think they firstly need to attend to the wild beasts within them, or else they may well offer a ministry that is artificial. The process of attending to our wild beasts makes us vulnerable and open and tolerant of wild beasts that we may find in others. They will also need to be full of respect, not seeing the sick person as the weak one, and them as the strong. After all, if we are aware of our own wild beasts, we are not likely to make ourselves out to be all triumphant and successful.

We come as 'equals' in the healing experience where the healing may well travel both ways. Aware of our own wild beasts, we will be delighted if the Spirit of God touches our wounded places as well. When it comes to praying for the sick person, we don't need eloquent words and effective techniques. We will simply need open and warm hearts, allowing the Spirit of God to give us that compassion that our Lord Jesus had in his healing encounters. It may well be that there will be times when we have no words. I have found that my prayers for healing with people are getting more and more childlike, and I think they are much more honest than they used to be. They can often be something like, 'Lord, it's so hard to see Dave suffering like this. Please help. Please heal him', and then there might be quite a long time of waiting in the presence of the love of God. I used to feel I had to fill all the time with words, but thankfully that silly nervousness is gradually being healed. I think it is kind, however, if there is a silence, to say something along the lines of 'Let's be quiet in the presence of the Lord who is with us to bring his healing'.

As I write I am becoming aware that what I am saying sounds rather too individualistic. It is time therefore to give some thought to healing in the context of community.

Story part 4:

The man who thought he could love

The man who thought he could love felt happy in this village. One evening he walked with Efah to the dry riverbank, as the heavy sun shimmered over the tall palm trees. It looked apologetic for the fierce heat it had given the village, scorching the ground and tiring the people. They sat on an old tree trunk washed up when the river was last full.

'How many paces is it to river from here now?' asked Efah. The man who thought he could love walked to the water's edge and returned. 'It is thirteen paces,' he said.

'Then it is getting very low and it may still be a long time before the rains come,' said Efah, and for the first time he saw anxiety in her face. He noticed it in the little turn of her lip, but it did not affect her warm sightless eyes.

'Are you worried, Efah?' he asked.

'For many years we have trusted Paska who is like the kindest of mothers, nurturing and feeding us.'

'Tell me about this Paska.'

'Paska is a wounded sheep.'

'A wounded sheep?' The man who thought he could love heard the way he said this. He heard the mockery,

the disrespect, the accusation of primitiveness, and he felt ashamed. But Efah only smiled and said, 'Yes, a wounded sheep, that is why he knows how to love.'

'Have you seen Paska, Efah?' he asked, and he felt better as he heard the respect in his voice.

'When our wise man with the brown robe came we only knew the gods who made us afraid. I remember the fear I saw in my parents' eyes. We worshipped the gods, but we felt cold. We called the wise man Raal, which in our language means "Beloved Child", because when he started talking to us about Paska he looked like the small children do when they are being loved. We wanted to know more about Paska because we so longed for the gods to love us. There were so many discussions by the village elders. You see, as we are a community, if one member of the village were to start worshipping Paska, we would all want to. So we all had to talk about it – the men and women, the old ones and the children. Then one night, one of our oldest women had a dream. She saw Paska in the dream. He was indeed a sheep and he came to her, and he knelt down before her. She saw tears in his eyes, like the drops of rain that form on the roofs of our huts when the heavy rain comes. They were tears of sorrow and joy, for he was weeping for all the sorrows she had ever known, and he was weeping for every joy that she had ever known, and the joy that he said would be hers in seven days. In the morning she asked the dream listeners to help her to understand the dream. Soon the village was in no doubt that she had seen Paska. Seven days after her dream she died. Raal buried her and on that day we began to love Paska. Of course he has loved us since before we were born.'

Efah's smile even outshone the setting sun, now dancing among the tall trunks of the palm trees. The man who thought he could love had never seen such a smile. It was a smile that revealed a depth of love that the man had never before seen, and the man who thought he could love felt loved like he had never known before. He knew that he could not love like this.

'My God is also a God of love,' said the man who knew he was being loved, but as he said this he felt an uncertainty in his heart as if he had just spoken a line of a creed that had never made its way from his lips to his heart, and he heard the hollowness.

'I know,' said Efah. 'But I think it is many paces to your river. I hear the sounds of other streams that have passed through dark cities and carry poison. I think you too have lost some of your sight. But I also hear the sound of rain. You see, Paska always sends the rain', and the smile spun out again as the sun tucked itself behind the silent hill and the man who knew he was loved was relieved that Efah could not see his twitching mouth, though she heard the sound of his swallowing.

'I must go,' he said, leaving Efah who was quickly being enfolded by the evening darkness – a darkness that held no fears for the girl who was blind. It held many for the man who could see.

Chapter 5

Healing in the Heart of Community

I first started writing this book a year ago. When I wrote the introduction I had just heard the news that my friend, Brother Ramon, who had been unwell for a while, had been diagnosed as being seriously ill with cancer. He invited me to take part in a Eucharist service to involve sacramental anointing for healing. I remember the service so clearly. I drove down to Worcestershire with anything but faith. I felt sad and tired at the thought of encountering another friend who had been afflicted by this disease which seemed to be cruelly picking off a number of my friends at random.

St Mary at the Cross, Glasshampton, is reached by driving up a long, winding and very bumpy track through the most beautiful Worcestershire fields, rich in their red soil. Eventually you reach the simple monastery building which was at one time Victorian stables, and within this welcoming home dwells a small Franciscan community. I was given a warm greeting at the door by one of the brothers who brought me up to date on Ramon's health. I was then somewhat surprised to see Ramon looking remarkably bubbly. When I had last seen him a few months before he was quite wearied by his illness, but on this occasion there was a radiance of faith that shone through him. As far as he was concerned, this was to be a service of faith and celebration. What an interesting dynamic – the patient: full of faith and joy; the one leading the ministry: doubting and fearful! Who was ministering to whom!

In correspondence before this service Ramon had written with characteristic wisdom, faith and honesty about his expectations at this service:

> What I would look for as a result of this anointing would be the will of God, and that could be expressed in (a) a complete healing; (b) gradual and partial physical healing; (c) strength and spiritual strength every moment, every day, whatever comes.

Lest that should be seen as in any way detached, Ramon added,

> I am a proud and independent fellow, and all this is not easy to carry, but I am also a simple and loving man, and I see my own creatureliness in human perspective. The Lord knows you and me through and through, our weaknesses and our hopes.

Ramon's wonderful mixture of faith and vulnerability helped me greatly as I prepared for this service. I was learning that I did not have to go to the service as Mr Radiant-Healer, but I could go as me, with my usual mixture of weakness and hope, and share with a friend in his own mixture of weakness and hope, simply coming to God to ask for his blessing. I was learning the importance of not demanding anything, but being open to whatever our God of love chose to give. The point I am labouring here is that my own inadequacy was really very irrelevant in this service of sacramental anointing, and Ramon in his weakness was helping to shift my eyes away from myself and on to the Lord Jesus who was becoming the focus of our attention.

I was a little nervous as I prepared to lead this service. I had attended services in this chapel before, but had never been the celebrant of the Eucharist before. I found myself momentarily distracted by fears of breaking some crucial codes of practice and saying the wrong things, but when I emerged from the vestry into the chapel I immediately felt surrounded by love. It sounds rather twee to talk about this surrounding of love, but I really cannot find another way of expressing it. For a start, there was Ramon sitting on a stool not far from the altar, and I was immediately aware of his kindness and goodness. But I was also aware of the community of people gathered in that chapel – a mixture of brothers in their Franciscan habits, and other friends whom Ramon had invited. I quickly lost my sense of awkwardness and was carried on a powerful sense of being complete in the context of this community. As the service proceeded I felt almost tangibly the gentle presence of the Lord, exhibited not least in the body language of the Franciscan brothers who were there. Don't ask me to describe it – I just felt it! After listening to the Gospel story of the woman of faith who touched the hem of Jesus' robe, we laid hands on our friend and brother, asking for the healing love and power of God to come and touch him in body, mind and spirit. We were aware that this sickness was not totally unconnected with the spiritual battle, for those living the hermit life know heights of glory and depths of darkness few of the rest of us know. Thus we prayed Celtic (remember Ramon is Welsh!) protection prayers as well as prayers for healing, and we bathed his forehead in the aromatic anointing oil and watched his forehead glisten in the warm August sunshine that filled the chapel. We sang our hymns of praise and broke the bread and drank the wine, reminding ourselves of the Servant of God whose suffering has opened the door of healing.

I realised in that service that though Ramon was the focus of the healing prayer, and I was the one leading the service, all of us were experiencing the healing touch of God. Certainly in the weeks that followed I felt something had changed in me. It has been hard to describe, but I think the healing that took place in that service was for me a greater freedom to be vulnerable. I left Glasshampton that evening not knowing how Ramon would be when I next saw him. Would God grant a complete healing, begin a gradual healing, or would he give Ramon the strength to prepare for the Great Journey? A week later I received a letter from him. In it he wrote,

Let me be down to earth and say that my pain has almost altogether disappeared, and that I feel better than I have for a good many weeks or even months. I had a session with my GP on Wednesday and told him that I was almost free from pain, and that I felt much, much better. I added that we had all been praying, and that prayer and medical care both contributed to the good results, but that I wasn't prepared to say what proportion was to be apportioned – and we both laughed, and we saw that something very important and wonderful was going on! You understand that I don't want to make flag-waving claims, but that with you I want to go on, simply, humbly, day by day, trusting the healing power to continue – so much of which was released during the Eucharist and anointing which spread much further abroad than my own body, mind and spirit.

Indeed, the healing had spread much further and was certainly touching my life. During the year the healing has continued. As I write this chapter, Ramon still knows times of discomfort, and we all know that he is mortal, and any time God may call any of us Home. But I think he would say this past year has been one of experiencing an extraordinary, mysterious and beautiful expression of the healing love of God.

Faith in community

As I reflect on this healing, one of the features that most impresses me is the community dimension of it. Although Ramon lives an enclosed life, his hermit life is lived very much in the context of community. At the service, we were very aware not only of the Franciscan community present in the chapel, but also of the many here and overseas who were praying for Ramon. During the service we read from the passage in James about anointing:

Are any among you sick? They should call for the elders of the church and have them pray over them, anointing them with oil in the name of the Lord. The prayer of faith will save the sick, and the Lord will

raise them up; and anyone who has committed sins
will be forgiven. Therefore confess your sins to one
another, and pray for one another, so that you may
be healed. The prayer of the righteous is powerful
and effective. (5:14–16)

My reading of the Gospels convinces me that it is Jesus'
intention that all Christian people should be engaged in
the ministry of healing.[1] However, this section from
James seems to suggest that it is the elders who do the
healing ministry. As I have puzzled over this, I have
come to see it in this way: I still believe all Christian
people should be open to pray for others to receive
healing. However, it is also appropriate to have a ritual
that demonstrates clearly the *corporate* nature of faith
and healing, and this ritual is anointing with oil. James
tells us that the elders are to do the anointing, and I
believe this is not because they are any better at doing
healing than other people, but because as elders they
have a representative role. That is, they engage in the
healing ministry not out of a sense of superiority, but
solidarity. They are the representatives of the whole
community, and the whole community should know that
this is the case. Thus when a member of the community
is sick, the elders go and do the anointing, but like
any sacrament, it is only effective if it is owned by the
community of faith. In the case of the healing service
with Brother Ramon, I was an 'elder', not of course of
the Franciscan community, but in the sense that I was
at that moment a representative of the community of
faith that included both members of the Franciscan
order and those outside of it. As an Anglican priest I

also came as representative of that part of the Church to which Ramon has chosen to belong.

The sacramental act of anointing therefore is supremely a community event. There will be times when someone is visiting a friend who is sick and it is entirely appropriate to offer to pray for healing for that person. These are the kinds of encounters that the seventy of Luke 10 were likely to meet – spontaneous and joyful outbursts, if you like, of the Holy Spirit. But alongside this spontaneous ministry there needs to be the corporate acts of faith such as the anointing with oil by the elders.

Warm air pockets

It is my belief that when we engage in these corporate acts, the spiritual health of the corporate group will have some influence. God has always called his people to dwell in community, whether it be the people of Israel in the Old Covenant, or the Body of Christ in the New. The so-called 'high priestly' prayer of Jesus in John 17 suggests that Jesus knew how hard it was going to be for us to achieve good levels of unity. The history of the Church over the past two thousand years, and a casual glance at the churches of today, suggest that we have still got a long way to go to achieve the kind of love for one another that Jesus prayed, and prays for. One of the reasons why we need to love one another is to develop the kind of community in which will flow the healing love of God. Can we really with all integrity hold a healing service for the sick when we are fighting each other tooth and nail in the church council meetings? Simplistic though it may sound, the more love there is in a church, the more likely there is to be healing. If we are finding it hard to see healings taking place in the life of our churches we may do no better than to look at the nature of our relationships with one another.

I can hear the sighs of despondency as I write. 'But Michael, you don't know *our* church. We will never achieve that level of loving one another in a month of Sundays. Are we therefore consigned to a life without healings?' To be honest, I don't often come across churches that are transparently communities of wonderful love! So much seems to militate against people loving one another. To name but a few: churches bound by dry dogmas that imprison people; powerful personalities who are determined to get their way; paranoid clergy who feel that anyone asking questions is undermining their authority; traditionalists who wish to keep faith a private matter; revivalists who develop a kind of 'survival of the fittest' spirituality, where the real heroes of faith are the spiritual athletes who win many for Christ, while the 'weak' labour under burdens of failure; and the list could go depressingly on. It seems to me that all churches have their draughty places and we should not be too upset by that even if it is disappointing. But, no matter how draughty they are, we can all foster pockets of warm air, where people become open and it is safe to love and be loved. This may be a particularly hospitable home or family; it may be a home group, a choir, the flower arrangers and any other group of people who are simply trying to live out the gospel command of loving one another. Of course, if such places become exclusive and judgemental of others, then we have only succeeded in creating another icy draught in the church, so there will be a real need to be open to the Spirit of God to direct us. But given that we can achieve a warm air pocket, then the likelihood is that the love of God will spread out from there, and in that warm environment healing will take place. A fire in the hearth, once it gets going, can heat a whole room.

Personally, I have found my home group to be a wonderful place of safety, and therefore an environment for healing. This is a church home group which my wife and I attend, and it meets once a week. Perhaps more than anything else, I appreciate our home group for the way in which it welcomes humanity, and it is a place where I do feel free to be myself. I don't think any of our group would claim it is perfect by any means. Like all gatherings of humans, it has its frustrations and failings. But I do thank God that it is by and large a place of refuge, a place where I can share both joys and sorrows, faith and doubts, hopes and fears.

Also, I have been part of a support group for the last ten years that has been a great strength to me. Led by Eric Delve, this group which we called 'The Rhino Club'[2] has met three times a year, and is made up of people who have a travelling ministry. There are many pitfalls and dangers in a travelling ministry, and there can be considerable loneliness. So it has been immensely helpful to come to this group, and I have been regularly impressed by the way each member of the group has been prepared to make himself vulnerable. I could testify to many occasions where the love and support of the friends in this group have opened the way for God's healing love to touch and restore me.

In all such small groups we will have to make allowances for different personalities. In most groups there will be a mixture of extraverts and introverts; there will be those who find it easy to share of themselves, and those who find it very hard. The more we get to know each other, the more our wounds are likely to be noticed, and our woundedness may well wound others. In every group there will be people we like and naturally feel close to, and there will be people with whom we may feel uncomfortable. The worst groups are those where the focus is only on the spiritual life. They can easily become unreal, and I have often seen people, confident in their ordinary lives, quickly de-skilled in a group if they think others in the group are better and more knowledgeable Christians.

Dietrich Bonhoeffer, before he was imprisoned by the Nazis and died a martyr's death at the end of the Second World War, experimented with community life and wrote about it in his book *Life Together*. In this he says,

> A purely spiritual relationship is not only dangerous but also an altogether abnormal thing. When physical and family relationships or ordinary associations, that is, those arising from everyday life with all its claims upon people who are working together, are not projected into the spiritual community, then we must be especially careful.[3]

The fact is that, when we come together, we come together as *humans*, and we share our humanity, not just our spirituality. If we come together just to share spiritual things then we will never be a group in which our humanity can find healing. Furthermore, we will always be a group that excludes those who are not

Christians, because the non-Christian or even the young Christian will always feel inferior.

A question I like to ask a home group is, 'If a member of your group were to lose their faith, would they still be welcome?' If the answer is 'no', then people are only members because they are there to share spiritually. If it is 'yes', then this indicates that the group values highly the relationships, and there is a sharing of common humanity. Of course, it is entirely appropriate for a church home group to want to share together matters to do with our faith. We will want to pray together and for one another, and read and study the Bible together, to worship and witness together. This is an outworking of the shared nature of our faith. The point is, what is the foundation? If the foundation is spiritual, then I am likely only to share with the group those things which I think are to do with my faith. The struggles I am having with my toddler may not seem very worthy compared with my friend who is on the verge of converting their neighbour. We can so easily become performance based. People will find it very hard to share what might be perceived as failures, especially if they feel other members of a group are going to make judgements on them. In both the groups I am part of I have seen Christian faith flourish and grow by people sharing their vulnerability.

I learned an important lesson about this in a group of which I was once a member, when one person stopped coming. At the time I and my wife were leaders of the group. I phoned the person whom I shall call Shirley. I remember the phone call well because there were so many silences at the other end of the line, and it con-

siderably tested my listening skills! I found it very hard
to know what was going on in the silences, but I really
did not want to intrude into them either. In the end, I
simply said, 'Well, Shirley, I just want you to know we
miss you and you will always be welcome' which
sounded rather feeble, but was true. My wife, Julia, then
saw her not long after that, and through her good listening, made more headway in understanding what was
happening for Shirley. It transpired that Shirley had
gone through a time of great doubt and felt she was no
longer a Christian. Her husband was not a Christian,
and I think he found church things pretty difficult. Julia
gave her much reassurance that we were there as friends
to support her, no matter what her spiritual condition
might be. It was wonderful when Shirley came to our
group again, because not only was she able to share her
difficulties of faith, but the members of the group made
very clear to her that even if she should never find faith
again, she was still very welcome and loved in the group.
As it happened, she did rediscover her faith, and it was
not unconnected with the love and prayers of the group.
Her husband also became much warmer. All this taught
me the importance of loving people for who they are, not
for the amount of faith they possess.

Another problem arises when people join our
churches and our small groups whom we really can't
stand! Here I am helped again by Jean Vanier who wrote
an article about fifteen years ago in a magazine called
Grass Roots. I came across this article while I was first
developing home groups in the church of which I was
the vicar in Kidderminster. We discovered it was not
that easy to get groups to flourish. Surely these little

Christian communities should work, I thought! Reading
Jean Vanier's article was most reassuring:

> When someone lives alone they can really think they
> are a saint. It is in living together, in relationship to
> people, that all kinds of feelings well up inside me –
> frustration, anger, fear. So community is really the
> place of the revelation of my darkness. None of us
> likes to discover our jealousies, our fears, our
> depression, our need to be loved, our desire to be
> better than others. Community is particularly
> painful because it is the place that reveals my
> wounds, my own inadequacies.[4]

We are back again to our theme of wild beasts and
angels. So many of us join the church home group
because we think that, by contrast to our 'secular' lives,
it will offer us a company of angels. It can be a terrible
shock to discover it is actually the place of wild beasts!
Even worse, it is disturbing to find it is the place where
I discover the wild beasts within me. Many have left
home groups and churches because they thought they
would be in the company of angels, and they were
shocked and disappointed to discover that they were in
the company of wild beasts.

The way through of course is to follow Jesus. It is he
who shows us how to sit down with the wild beasts and
to draw from the angelic resources of heaven. If our
churches and our home groups are to be truly places
of growth and healing, then they must provide places of
safety where I can bring my wild beasts into the presence
of Jesus. It is probably the most irritating person rather

than the most saintly who will help me to grow. In the same article, Jean Vanier writes,

> The precise message of Jesus that renders it different from every other message, philosophy and spirituality, is 'Love your enemies'. A disciple of Jesus Christ is one who loves the enemy. The enemy is not the national enemy or the class enemy; the enemy is the one who threatens me, the one I block off from, the one who has to open his mouth for me to know that what he says is wrong.

I have to acknowledge that my humanity will find some people difficult. They will be like wild beasts for me – they will threaten me; they bring the worst out in me; I want to flee from them, not sit next to them in a cosy home group! And yet, that 'wild beast' may well have the potential to be an angel in disguise. They may be the person who can cause me to grow in a way that no close friend could cause me to grow. If I will but listen to myself, to why I fear that person, why I find them difficult, I will begin a journey of self-exploration, into which can come the life-bearing Spirit to make her nest and breed her young. Such miracles take place all the time, and if this is not healing, then I don't know what is!

Community, sexuality and healing

One 'wild beast' that most Christians are very anxious about is sexuality. For hundreds of years in the Christian tradition we have found it very hard to bring sexuality and spirituality to a meeting place. The Church has inherited the Augustinian suspicion of sex. To make things harder we live in a world (in the West) which is sex mad. So I walk out of a sex-mad world into a 'sex-free' church, and this makes for deep confusion. To illustrate, think of the following scenario for a heterosexual man going to church. Everything gets off to a good start: he is taken up to heaven because he is singing his favourite hymn. His spirit is lifted up. But then at the end of the hymn, the rather attractive young lady in front of him turns round to sit down and he notices her low-cut dress, a dress that clearly was not designed by Augustine's tailor. Suddenly there is dreadful confusion! One moment he could not be holier if he tried, the next moment he is all too aware of the lusts of the flesh. What does he do? He either tries to pretend to himself he did not notice, and remains in the happy warmth of holiness he experienced in the singing of the hymn. Or he issues a rebuke to his flesh and does battle with the enemy. Or he sinks into despair and thinks to himself that he will never be free of the old flesh that regularly drags him down.

I never cease to be encouraged by St Paul in Romans 7 and 8. I am so grateful for his utter honesty in chapter 7, in which he discusses the problems of 'the flesh', and very likely he is talking about sexual temptations here. You can sense his feelings growing stronger and he writes,

> I do not understand my own actions. For I do not do what I want, but I do the very thing I hate. Now if I do what I do not want, I agree that the law is good. But in fact it is no longer I that do it, but sin that dwells within me. For I know that nothing good dwells within me, that is, in my flesh. I can will what

is right, but I cannot do it. For I do not do the good I want, but the evil I do not want is what I do. Now if I do what I do not want, it is no longer I that do it, but sin that dwells within me. So I find it to be a law that when I want to do what is good, evil lies close at hand. For I delight in the law of God in my inmost self, but I see in my members another law at war with the law of my mind, making me captive to the law of sin that dwells in my members. Wretched man that I am! Who will rescue me from this body of death? (7:15–24)

You sense his anguish as he writes this. Here is this great visionary leader, pioneering the Christian gospel, achieving extraordinary things for the Kingdom of God, admired by Christians all over Palestine and Asia Minor, yet despite the wonderful working of the grace of God on his life, he is still aware of the wild beasts within, which cause him to do the very things he hates doing, and he sees sinful ways in his own body. Oh, who will rescue him? He answers his own question:

Thanks be to God through Jesus Christ our Lord! So then, with my mind I am a slave to the law of God, but with my flesh I am a slave to the law of sin. There is therefore now no condemnation for those who are in Christ Jesus. For the law of the Spirit of life in Christ Jesus has set you free from the law of sin and of death. (7:25–8:2)

Paul has been honest about the wild beasts within him, but because he is equally honest about the angel of hope, such acknowledgement of the wild beast does not lead to condemnation. There is enormous hope in the Spirit of God, and the rest of chapter 8 describes the wonderful and mysterious working of the Spirit of God which raised Jesus from the great beast of death, and comes in power to the wild and wounded places of our humanity. I see in Romans 7 and 8 a wonderful balance of honesty about the wild beasts within us, and a great sense of hope in the power of the Spirit to transform us.

We should not be surprised therefore to find ourselves thrown between temptation and revelation. As humans we will have those moments when we will be caught up into the heavenlies, and other moments when we feel dragged down by our own sinfulness. One does not deny the existence or validity of the other. But if we want the power of the Spirit in our lives, then we will have to own those places of the weakness of the flesh, and a safe context for this is the small group in which there is a commitment to love and support one another even in our failings.

One area of sexuality that has received much attention recently is the issue of homosexuality. I find all the debates and discussions about homosexuality in the Church painful and often confusing. Those at either end of the debate often come over as angry, dark and very unloving. I think perhaps we find the debate so difficult precisely because for centuries we have avoided facing the wild beasts of sexuality in our own humanity. I see many people, particularly those who campaign against homosexuals, displaying signs of denying their own sexuality. As a result anger rises up, and perhaps part of that anger is a sense of frustration that we, as Christian people, feel so vulnerable discussing issues of sexuality, because it is an area we have consistently avoided.

In the midst of these debates, there is a group of people who have to exist a kind of life in hiding. They are aware of their orientation and preferences for their own sex, but they would never dare admit this in their churches. They may have 'come out' amongst some friends, or in the safety of communication on the Internet, but never in their church. I think of one person who has talked confidentially to me about her orientation, and also about how much she loves her church. But she also tells of how her minister makes aggressive statements in the pulpit against homosexuals, and how many in her church would share his views. She therefore has to hide this part of her humanity, for, she feels, if she were to share it, it would be viewed as a threatening wild beast (even that *she* might become a threatening wild beast) that would savage many in the church. I wonder how many people who are aware of homosexual orientation, are hiding secretly in their churches hoping no one will discover them, and feeling personally bruised every time there is an attack on homosexuality from the pulpit or in the Christian press. The issue is far from straightforward. Thank God, in the debates, there are many good, just and wise people helping us to discern God's will. But in the midst of the debates there is a real need to remember the individuals, and to create safe places for people to share parts of their inner lives that are suffering because of isolation and feared rejection.

In an age when there has been a terrible breakdown of our sense of community, we have a wonderful gift to offer our society, which is the simple, vulnerable gift of groups of people who are committed to living out their humanity together under the healing influence of the Holy Spirit.

The man who thought he was not alone

The man who thought he was not alone was surprised by the fear he saw in Efah.

'If the rains do not come soon, we will have to leave,' she said. 'None of us want to leave here. When the cool evening comes, we are meeting with the elders to talk and pray.' She looked up towards the man who thought he was not alone and turned her head revealing great tenderness, and said, 'Tell me. What do you do in your land when you feel afraid?'

The man who thought he was not alone thought of the many times that he had felt afraid, yet never dared to show it. He remembered the fear caused by his father's rage, the fear caused by the threat of bankruptcy, the fear he felt in church when he had to go door-to-door evangelising. But he could not bring himself to mention any of these to Efah, so he said, 'People who believe in God would pray, of course.'

'Yes,' said Efah and smiled. 'So do we.' Then she looked at him again and said, 'But you have not told me what you do when you are afraid', and she looked almost hurt that he had avoided her question. He still could not bring himself to admit his fears to this young girl, for he was the one to strengthen her, not the other

way round. He looked at her sightless eyes gazing at a point just to the right of his head, and felt oddly relieved that those tender eyes were not fixed on him. 'If someone in my country is worried or afraid . . .' he started.

'Why do you say "if"?' asked Efah. 'Do you mean there are some people who do not have fear?'

'No . . . no,' the man stuttered, 'I mean, I'm sure everyone feels fear at times', but as the man spoke he heard the confusion in his voice, and in that confusion he heard his lack of hearing, and he knew that Efah had heard it too.

'Do you have friends?' asked Efah.

'I have many friends in my church,' said the man who thought he was not alone.

'And are they friends of the heart?' asked Efah, turning her head to one side as if to hear the answer more clearly. The man who thought he was not alone felt something uneasy within him. It was a feeling he did not want to own, and he pushed his way past it hurriedly by saying, 'Yes, yes, I'm sure . . .' and he heard the stuttering again. It felt like there was a searchlight on a part of him that had rested in darkness for many years. He turned the light off by shifting the attention to Efah: 'You have not told me what you do when you are afraid.'

'You will see tonight,' she said. 'You must come to our meeting.' Efah walked back to her little home, and thought about all that the man who thought he was not alone had said by not answering her question. The man felt fear in his stomach. He did not like feeling it. He did not even know what it was about. He saw fear

in Efah, and that made him afraid. He felt afraid about the drought, and feared having a parched throat. The fear made him feel alone, but he was not ready yet to know this.

The people of the village met late in the evening when the dark was very dark, and each torch blazed bright in the companionship room, and the flickering light emphasised the lines and grooves on the faces of the elders.

'This is a time for the open heart,' said an old man whose eyes were the kindest that the man who thought he was not alone had ever seen.

A young mother leaned forward and said, 'Then I will tell you that I am very afraid. I have lived in this village all my life, and never has the water been so low. I am afraid it will be too stale to drink. I am afraid that my children will become ill. I need you to hold my heart.'

'And I,' said a man who had spent the day placing precious drops of water around his shrivelling plants, 'feel afraid, and I feel sad to see my plants drooping so, and when I look at my plants, I feel my spirit also drooping.' The man who thought he was not alone listened to many voices, each telling of their fears and sorrows. 'They need so much help,' he thought, and felt he knew why he had come to this village.

The old man who had spoken first said, 'It is now time to come to Paska. Tell me, who has listened to Paska?'

'I have,' said a young child, and came forward to stand near the old man, and both their faces were lit up by the fluttering light of the torch. 'And I know he is afraid too.'

'Yes,' said the old man, 'if we have heard this, then it is time for us to be still in his presence', and his voice drifted over the group of friends gathered together in the companionship room, and when the last memories of it disappeared into the night, a silence came; a silence was given. A sacred silence; a silence of love; a silence of pain understood; a silence of desperate prayers heard; a silence of knowledge; a silence of silence. In the midst of the silence, the man who thought he was not alone heard his own heart, and as he surveyed this heart he saw that it was the host of many stories, stories to do with his brother being preferred, stories of finding friends in strength, but being ashamed in weakness, and worst of all, stories of fearing that God was too good, too big, too perfect. He was touching his loneliness, and dared call it by name. As he did so, the old man who had spoken first came silently to him and held him close, and held him tight.

'You are learning about the open heart,' he whispered, and the man who thought he had not been alone, now knew he was not alone, for his open heart was safe, and in the safety of the old man's arms, his open heart gave voice to its pain and joy, and the silence of the companionship room became the cradle for the infant cry.

Chapter 6

Healing and Hope

The theme 'wild beasts and angels' comes from the account of Jesus in the wilderness right at the start of his ministry. The two images of beast and angel come together again towards the end of his earthly ministry, and the link is significant. At the beginning of the Gospel accounts of Jesus' ministry we find him in a wilderness; towards the end we find him in a garden, and we need now to explore this garden story a little more closely.

In Luke's account of Jesus in the Garden of Gethsemane before his arrest, we find again the themes of testing, angels and wild beasts (Luke 22:39–51). Whereas the first testing took place in a barren wilderness, this time it is in a luscious olive grove; on the first occasion he was utterly alone, this time he is in the company of his friends. And yet the circumstances are such that the garden is like a barren wasteland, and his friends, though nearby, have removed themselves from him by going to sleep. Before his ministry began he had to go through the temptation in the desert; before the mighty act of cross and resurrection he had to go through the temptation in the garden.

These themes of garden and desert are tremendously

powerful in the Bible. The Bible starts with a story of a garden – a garden from which humans are exiled. We then have the followers of God in the desert before they cross the Jordan and enter the garden of the Promised Land. They then lose the garden and are taken as slaves through the desert. In Babylon they try to sing their songs in a strange land while their faith is kept alive by holding on to promises delivered by the prophet Isaiah, that there will be in the desert a highway, a way back to the fertile home.[1] Finally the future hope is about a garden, the Garden of Paradise, a Persian word that literally means 'exquisite garden'.

So here is Jesus in the garden and it reminds us of the first Adam in the Garden of Eden who faced the terrible temptation which resulted in exile. John Henry Newman caught this so well in his amazing poetic work 'The Dream of Gerontius' which Elgar set to music. Gerontius dies and he arrives somewhat bewildered in Paradise. However an angel comes to assist him and long discussions proceed to help him understand the nature of life and death. I love Elgar's setting, which rises to a wonderful crescendo when the 'choir of angelicals' lift their voices in great triumph as they sing a hymn which is familiar to many of us:

> Praise to the Holiest in the height,
> And in the depth be praise;
> In all his works most wonderful,
> Most sure in all his ways.
>
> O loving wisdom of our God!
> When all was sin and shame,

A second Adam to the fight,
And to the rescue came.

O wisest love! that flesh and blood,
Which did in Adam fail,
Should strive afresh against the foe,
Should strive and should prevail.

Newman has caught in poetry St Paul's theme that Jesus was the 'second Adam'.[2] Just as in the first garden, the first Adam engaged in a mighty wrestling match with Satan, so in the second garden, the second Adam engages in another great wrestle with Satan. Whereas the first time round Adam fails, this time Jesus, fully human and yet also divine, succeeds – he strives and prevails.

In Luke's Gospel we have this sequence: Jesus eats his Passover meal with his disciples; there is a dispute about who should be regarded as the greatest, and Jesus teaches them about serving; Jesus warns Simon Peter that Satan has demanded to sift the disciples like wheat; Peter swears undying loyalty to Jesus; Jesus warns them that there might be conflict; they go out to the Mount of Olives.

Once we arrive at the Mount of Olives, there is a great sense of tension, and Jesus says to his disciples, 'Pray that you may not come into the time of trial', language reminiscent of the wilderness trial. He is making clear that this is going to be a moment of terrible testing. Then Jesus goes a little distance from them and prays to his Father. The following passage is particularly interesting, not least because it does not appear in some versions of Luke's Gospel!

> Then an angel from heaven appeared to him and gave him strength. In his anguish he prayed more earnestly, and his sweat became like great drops of blood falling down to the ground. (22: 43–4)

Why doesn't it appear in some of the early versions? It is either because the event did not happen and someone made up the idea and added it, or it *did* happen and for some reason a scribe left it out when he was writing out the Gospel. I suppose we will never know, but I sometimes wonder if a scribe, copying this Gospel out, may have been so astonished by this part of the event that he could not bring himself to write it out. Perhaps he was affronted by the fact that the humanity of Jesus is so exposed. We have a glimpse here of a moment in the life of Jesus when we see in sharp contrast the activity of both wild beast and angel. This is another moment in his life when his humanity is so fully revealed in all its potential weakness. For those who prefer a more spiritual Jesus, this time of testing is truly uncomfortable and even offensive.

Luke tells us that Jesus was 'becoming more earnestly in an agony'. He uses the word *agonia*, which is a Greek word for someone fighting a battle with utter fear. This was the wild beast that assaulted Jesus in the garden. It was his almost paralysing fear of what was to come. The pressure of the fear was so powerful in him that the stress was literally causing the blood vessels on the forehead to rupture. He begged his Father to take this cup of suffering from him, and yet in the midst of the fear he remained utterly resolved to do his Father's will. In the evening shadows of the garden this titanic struggle took place, as hard a struggle as the temptations in the wilderness. And as in the wilderness, the Father in heaven sent an angel to give him strength. Despite the fact that Jesus could have called legions of angels to his aid at any time, there are only two moments in the Gospels when we are told he has direct contact with the angels. Both times are in times of great testing. Both times the angels are there to strengthen him. And how did the angel strengthen him? As with the angel in the wilderness, we do not know, and yet I cannot help but think the angel was reminding Jesus of the Father's love: 'You are his beloved Son'. As Jesus in his humanity let the knowledge and experience of the Father's love sink deep into his heart and soul, he was given the foundation to endure the terrible suffering that was to come.

There is another link with the wilderness story. In the Judean wilderness we are told that *the* wild beast, Satan, tempted Jesus. He poked and prodded into Jesus' humanity, trying to force submission and sin, but Jesus was resolute in his defiance. In the garden, Satan comes to Jesus again. This time, Satan comes in the form of a person; he comes in the form of a friend. Luke tells us that 'Satan entered into Judas called Iscariot, one of the twelve' (22:3). In whatever way we understand this, the fact is that Judas' soul had somehow been invaded by the dark presence of Satan, and now Satan in Judas comes to Jesus in the garden and actually dares to kiss our Lord. This kiss immediately unleashes violence in the garden and the process of the unjust trial, humiliation and crucifixion has begun.

The terrible thing about this testing in the garden is that everything is so disguised. A serene garden disguises a fiery wilderness trial. A company of friends disguises the loneliness of Jesus. A friend coming to kiss Jesus disguises the great beast seeking to devour him. The garden testing is one which is more sophisticated and more sinister. It is the testing where outwardly all looks well, but inwardly an agony is going on. In this story, once again, we see our Lord Jesus at ease with both the wrestlings of his own humanity and the resources of heaven to help him.

In the way that he faces his *agonia*, Jesus is showing us the way for us as we have to face our own fears. The disciples had not explored their own humanity as Jesus had. As they watched their Lord enter his suffering, they could not bear it. They caught the sniff of fear in that night air and they did what most humans instinctively do in the face of fear – they hid. Peter had failed to look at that part of his humanity that could not be a superhero. He had failed to discover that inside himself there was a man who, when the pressure was on, would not die with his master, but would deny him to save his own skin. He, like the others, hid, and the way they hid was to sleep.

The problem with hiding is that you do not attend to the wild beasts within, and if you do not attend to the wild beasts within, sooner or later they will rise up and attack someone near you. This is what happened to Peter. When he saw the soldiers, the wild beasts of fear and rage rose up in him and he attacked Malchus, slicing off his ear with his sword. Later in the story, Peter had more to discover about the wild beasts within him, as with oaths he denied his master. By the end of that terrible day, as his master was uttering his great and terrible scream on the cross, Peter was in no doubt about the true content of his own humanity as his soul entered a dark night of bitter weeping.

Wonderfully, the story did not end there. For the great wild beast of death was gloriously and wonderfully defeated by the angelic message of resurrection on Easter morning and Peter, now knowing and owning his fallible humanity, is reinstated by the risen Lord. However, the appearance of the risen Jesus does not inevitably make our lives one continuous success story.

Tremblings and ecstasy

I love all the accounts of the resurrection appearances, but perhaps the one that fascinates me most is Mark's account. The ending of Mark's Gospel is a literary puzzle and people have debated long and hard about its authentic conclusion. Translations of this final chapter will usually contain a footnote explaining that some ancient authorities end the chapter at verse 8, whilst others end it at verse 20. In the various debates, the assumption is usually made that Mark could not possibly have ended his Gospel with the verse:

> So they went out and fled from the tomb, for terror and amazement had seized them; and they said nothing to anyone, for they were afraid. (Mark 16:8)

Most scholars are agreed that Mark's authentic work ended here. It is generally reckoned that he had written more but that somehow or other the authentic ending got lost, and what we have in verses 9 following is a version written by someone else. The fourth-century scholars Eusebius and Jerome acknowledge that these crucial final verses are missing in all the best Greek manuscripts known to them. The section beginning in verse 9 was regarded as canonical, but written in a hand in sympathy with but different to Mark's. One possible explanation for the disappearance of the ending is that the original scroll was so well read that the ending got ragged and torn and in time the final part fell off.

Few people believe that Mark intended to conclude his Gospel at verse 8. The idea that Mark would end his great Gospel with news of fleeing, terrified, tongue-tied disciples seems to most people highly improbable. This is not exactly confidence-boosting stuff! However, the more I think about this, the more I find myself identifying with the few people who think that Mark *did* intend to finish here. The reason for this is that I believe he was trying to say something very profound to us about the life of the disciple who is following the risen Lord. He is, I believe, acknowledging something important about our humanity.

Let us suppose that Mark did intend to end his Gospel with this abrupt ending: what was he trying to communicate? An important clue comes in the final two words that he uses. He tells us that the women who fled from the tomb were seized with 'terror' and 'amazement'. In the Greek, these words are *tromos* and *ecstasis*. The first word speaks of a nervous awe, and the second speaks of utter ecstatic joy. Interestingly, Mark uses these two words only one other time in his Gospel and it is when, in chapter 5, he is describing the story of another resurrection, the story of the raising of Jairus' daughter. In this story, Mark tells us that Jesus is stopped on his way to Jairus' home by a woman who has been suffering for twelve years with a haemorrhage. She creeps up behind Jesus in the crowd and secretly touches his robe in the hope that somehow she will be healed. Wonderfully, the moment she contacts his robe she is healed, and no doubt she hopes to beat a hasty and happy retreat through the crowd. But before she can get away, Jesus stops in his tracks and asks who has touched him. Mark tells us that this woman then comes to Jesus 'in fear and trembling' (v. 33). He uses this word *tremo*, from which the word *tromos* is derived. The trembling is different from the fear, though related. It is a physical manifestation of an inner emotion. What is the emotion? Certainly it must be related to fear, but in this story we can reasonably guess that it would have contained a number of feelings to do with a sheer sense of awe that she had encountered a very great power, together with an anxiety as to quite what this powerful person was going to do with her now she was owning up to the fact that she was the one who had touched his robe.

The other word, *ecstasis*, comes right at the end of the story. When Jairus' daughter is raised from the dead, we are told that the crowd were overcome with amazement, *ecstasis*. It is a profoundly joyful recognition that there is someone in the world who has the power to invade the desperate and tragic sorrows of our lives and bring all that we hope for into being. It is these two experiences, *tromos* and *ecstasis*, that are present in the resurrection experience. Both are present – one does not negate the other; they co-exist.

Perhaps the longer ending of Mark was written by someone who needed much more certainty. The longer ending is definitely more confident. In this account we have Jesus upbraiding doubting disciples, we have the call to go into the world to preach the gospel, we have the promise of a tongue-speaking, demon-casting, snake-handling, poison-drinking, sick-healing Christian community. The last verse of this section refers not to nervous trembling, but to miraculous signs. Whilst I have no doubt that Jesus did teach and do all that is related in the longer ending of Mark, I wonder about the motives of the one who wrote it. A possible scenario is that Mark was one who had confidently allowed the risen Jesus to lead him to acknowledge his own wild beasts within his humanity. Perhaps the longer version was written by someone who had not yet explored their own wild beasts of fear and trembling and could not cope with a Gospel ending with such vulnerable humanity.

Wounded Lamb

We shall probably never know the truth about the ending of Mark's Gospel, but we can at least see in this a glimpse of the truth that the presence of the risen Jesus did not mean an immediate escape from the pains and problems of our earth-bound humanity. Neither was the resurrection about escaping from our humanity into an existence which prefers spirit to matter. No, the fact is that there are more references to the physical nature of Jesus' body after his resurrection than before. We have already seen the significance of the physicality of the risen Jesus in Chapter 2. One of the fascinating features of this physical risen body is the fact that it still bears the marks of the wounds that killed it. Even more astonishing is the thought that this same body ascended into heaven and, we must assume, still bears the scars of his wounded humanity. We think of heaven as a place of complete absence of the knowledge of suffering, and yet on the very throne of heaven is a wounded Saviour. The nineteenth-century hymn writer, M. Bridges, captures this so well in the wonderful hymn 'Crown Him with many crowns'. This is a hymn about the vulnerable yet glorious Lamb on a throne. The hymn includes the verse,

> Crown Him the Lord of Love,
> Behold His hands and side,
> Those wounds yet visible above,
> In beauty glorified.
> No angel in the sky,
> Can fully bear that sight,
> But downward bends his burning eye,
> At mysteries so bright.

Bridges helps us to see that it is the marks of his suffering that point Jesus out as the Lord of Love. His wounds proclaim to the whole company of heaven that he has loved humankind so much that he has suffered and died for us. As he now reigns in heaven he still carries suffering humanity in his heart. In the next verse, Bridges goes on to talk about the power of Christ who reigns that wars may cease:

> His reign shall know no end,
> And round His piercéd feet,

> Fair flowers of Paradise extend,
> Their fragrance ever sweet.

This verse makes contact with the agony of warfare that has been such a source of suffering in the last century, where far, far too many bodies have been pierced by sword, spear, bullet and bomb. And yet in heaven there is a Prince of Peace around whose pierced body grow the fair flowers of Paradise. Some will find this literally too flowery, but there is a profound truth in this concept. It is this wonderful knowledge that in heaven there is a human who was killed by the violence of this world, yet who came through with triumph. In his place of triumph he still carries the scars, thereby signalling that despite residing in the glorious chambers of heaven he understands the wounds of the cruel corridors of this suffering world.

The reigning wounded Lamb of God gives us enormous heart. It gives us heart because it tells us that there is a place in this existence where suffering and glory meet. There is someone who both weeps with our weeping but also provides a song of hope and joy. The image of the reigning ruling Lamb does not suddenly give us an easy-to-follow solution to the problem of suffering. But it does give us hope.

C. S. Lewis tackles the paradox of suffering and hope in the Narnia story, *The Magician's Nephew*. In the story Digory, the young boy, is taken to witness the creation of all things and he enjoys Narnia in its pre-fallen Paradise. Here he meets the great Aslan, the lion who is the symbolic figure of Christ. At the beginning of the story we hear that Digory's mother is seriously sick and understandably Digory is hurting and afraid. Despite the glory of all that he witnesses in this Narnian paradise, he finds his mind returning to his mother, and he finally plucks up courage to speak to Aslan about it. He comes with a good deal of fear and trembling, not knowing quite how this great lion will feel about this young mortal asking him for help. And so with tears and stutters he blurts out:

> 'But please, please – won't you – can't you give me something that will cure Mother?' Up till then Digory had been looking at the Lion's great front feet and the huge claws on them; now in his despair, he looked up at its face. What he saw surprised him as much as anything in his whole life. For the tawny face was bent down near his own and (wonder of wonders) great shining tears stood in the Lion's eyes. They were such big, bright tears compared with Digory's own that for a moment he felt as if the Lion must really be sorrier about his Mother than he was himself.
>
> 'My son, my son,' said Aslan, 'I know. Grief is great...'[3]

C.S. Lewis has caught this so well. In Paradise there is one who weeps for us because he knows that grief is great. In the story, Aslan does provide healing for Digory's mother, but not before he has shown how much he shares in Digory's pain and grief. I believe that C.S. Lewis is conveying an important truth here – that the compassion that motivated Jesus while he was in his incarnate form on earth, is still very much part of him. The wounds that mark his body in heaven are evidence that he is one who truly can say 'I know, I know' and who feels the pains of human suffering. He has not forgotten the ferocity of the wild beasts. But at the same time he *is* in heaven. He is among the angels. He is the one who is able to reach out with the power of heaven and heal, restore and forgive.

The relationship between glorious heaven and wounded earth is not an easy one to comprehend, but it is helped by the understanding that in heaven the wounds of earth are understood, and that on earth the power of heaven is released. I remember being very aware of this when the terrible tragedy happened at Dunblane. Not only were we filled with grief for the children who died in the shooting, but all of us who were parents at the time, who had dropped off our children at our primary schools that same morning, shuddered with horror as we realised that a gunman could have come into our schools and murdered our children. For me, an added dilemma was the discovery that a number of these children were from Christian families. Every day I pray for my children and, aware that we do live in a violent world, I pray for their safety. I have always taken comfort from the many promises of protection that we have in the Bible. In Psalm 91 I read, 'For he will command his angels concerning you to guard you in all your ways', and thank God that in this violent world we have angels to protect us and our children. I have always found this such a comfort. But then I hear of children, whose parents have read and trusted Psalm 91, being apparently unprotected as their young lives are snatched away by violence. I remember watching the terrible scenes outside the school and among all the floral tributes I noticed the words 'Angels' made with flowers. For a while I felt such anger towards the angels. Surely they failed in their duties to protect our young. What use were angels if they could not protect us? In my anger and grief, I wrote a poem which in the end helped me greatly to resolve in my own soul this paradox.

ANGELS AT DUNBLANE

Where were you when evil visited Class Primary 1?
Where you not alert, on guard
While the innocents fumbled with gym shoes
And chattered contentedly, unaware of the darkness?
  When the violent sounds of pistol
Stole so many precious lives
Could you not shield with mighty wings
And slay the evil?
Could you not restrain such deadly demons
That carry the stench of hell into such heavenly
  sweetness?
*These Gethsemane questions are beyond our
  knowledge*
But know this:
*That when those sweet flowers fell shedding
  crimson petals*
We were there
Gathering such a bouquet as heaven seldom saw.
*We overflew cold Calvary and heard again the cry
  of desolation,*
Yet also saw the open tomb
And we danced together with those young
In the glory fields of Paradise.

> *One of us looked back to those bleak school gates*
> *And saw white flowers arranged with caring hand*
> *To bear the name, 'Angels'.*
> *We marvelled that we could be honoured thus*
> *To be compared to such noble lives.*

Sickness and heaven

When we are with someone who is very seriously ill, we are forced to turn our attention to heaven. One way or another heaven comes into the picture. Some of the friends to whom I have dedicated this book have known the healing power of heaven break in and touch them with healing grace; for others, the pathway to healing has been one that has led them to enter heaven through the gateway of death.

John and Jacqui have been good friends to me and my family for over ten years. A couple of years before we met, John had an extraordinary experience that set the agenda for the rest of his life. He was at a prayer meeting in a farmhouse in his home village of Snitterfield, near Stratford on Avon. The farmhouse and adjoining buildings were in a very poor state. Unexpectedly, as John was enjoying being part of this prayer meeting, he was suddenly transported in the spirit and saw the farm buildings from an aerial view. He saw the buildings totally refurbished and transformed into a Christian retreat centre. He was a young Christian and quite shaken to have had such a vision. He shared this with Jacqui, his vicar and the local Christians who all felt that this was indeed a vision given by the Lord and they must begin to respond in faith. Soon a Trust was formed and remarkably sufficient money was given to buy the farm and its buildings, and work began to build the Christian centre. In time, John and Jacqui moved in at the invitation of the Trustees and little by little the vision became realised. John and Jacqui's steadfastness of vision impressed us all, as they persisted in faith through those frustrating times when nothing could move because there was no money, and a multitude of delays and problems frustrated the plans. But press on they did and from the broken-down old farm buildings, the Red Hill Christian Centre arose.

In the midst of all of this, John and I visited the Holy Island of Lindisfarne together for a few days during a very blustery and damp March. This was another time of revelation for both of us. We became very aware of the proximity of heaven as we strode around the island in the gale and rain, and felt strangely close to Cuthbert and Aidan who had dwelt on the island many hundreds of years previously and who now prayed for us in heaven. This experience was one of the seeds that contributed to the emergence of the Community of Aidan and Hilda which is devoted to interpreting the spirituality of the early Celtic Church for today's society.

Two years ago John developed back pain that in time was diagnosed to be caused by cancer. All of us who knew and loved John were greatly shocked and a number of us prayed for his healing. Although John was never fully well again, he did have a time of some remission. For him and Jacqui it was not an easy time, as they struggled to know whether God was going to bring about a full healing or whether he was calling John home. No matter how wonderful heaven looks, the strength of human love is such that it always feels better to have a loved one here on earth where you can hug them, talk to them, laugh with them, cry with them and simply know their near presence. So, in our humanity, we desperately looked to God for him to cure John and restore him to full health.

In April I took my annual retreat at Glasshampton Monastery. It was good to be there again, and especially good to see my friend Brother Ramon looking so well. However, while I was there I received the news that John was very poorly. As I took John into my evening prayers in the quiet monastery chapel I sensed that he was close to death. I left my retreat and went straight to Snitterfield, to visit him. It was an extraordinarily poignant scene. The building work on the farm buildings was almost complete. They had been transformed beyond all recognition. A true resurrection work had been done. And yet in the heart of this resurrection story, lying in his bed in the farmhouse was John, with his mortal life slipping away little by little. In the course of our conversation John told me with characteristic openness and faith that he was ready to embark on the Great Journey. Within two days of that meeting he was indeed journeying from this world, and we all felt, as he entered Paradise, he would have heard so clearly the words from his Friend and Master, 'Well done, good and faithful servant'.

We buried John under a great tree in Snitterfield Churchyard. It was a blustery, showery day, and as they lowered him into the earth, a squall blew up and a shower burst upon us. It reminded me so much of that day we had walked across Lindisfarne in such similar conditions, and it felt as if John was telling us that the

Wild Spirit was very much with him – and with us. In those moments there seemed to be very little space between heaven and earth.

Such experiences of death and loss sear us and make us very aware of our humanity. It is very difficult to hide from the wild beasts of anger and fear that rise up in response to the pain of grief. And yet, even through our tears, we are often given visions of glory that sustain us. I am learning, little by little, that fundamental to the healing ministry is an acceptance of my humanity and an acknowledgement of my own mortality. When we lose someone we love it reminds us of our mortality. Sickness reminds us of our own mortality.

Last Christmas I went to the Midnight Mass in Derby Cathedral. It was a wonderful service full of light and hope. But the service was spoiled for me by my humanity – specifically a back pain that I had had for a couple of months that made sitting very uncomfortable. During the service I found myself becoming quite morose about it, in contrast to the lightness of the service. I kept on thinking how John's cancer had started in his back, and I tried to ignore those little probing questions, 'Just what is causing this back pain?' After I had taken my Communion, I decided to listen to God about it, to let him speak a word of reassurance, to bring me back to my senses and stop me from being unnecessarily miserable and melodramatic. I felt I heard him, quite clearly as it happened, refer me to a hymn number. I was given just the number – 402. I picked up the hymn-book and turned to 402. It was a hymn by Richard Baxter, the first three verses of which are:

Lord, it belongs not to my care
Whether I die or live;
To love and serve thee is my share,
And this thy grace must give.

If life be long, I will be glad
That I may long obey;
If short, yet why should I be sad
To welcome endless day?

Christ leads me through no darker rooms
Than he went through before;
He that into God's Kingdom comes
Must enter by this door.

I didn't know whether to laugh or cry! Was God telling me that my days left on this earth were short? For a moment I really did feel frightened and the wild beast took some subduing. However, I realised that I was meant to listen to a deeper message. 'Lord, it belongs not to my care, whether I live or die' – this is what I had to grasp. Of course I want to live – I have much to live for, but what I heard God saying to me through that hymn was that I must not try to tell him how long I should live. I heard God telling me, very gently and lovingly, that my purpose is to love and serve God and others. If we make our main purpose a grim desire to hang on to life, then we have missed the point. I felt the word of God 'piercing through bone and marrow' and challenging (not for the first time) my need to control. I wanted to be in control of my life, my health and my death, but I am learning that actually this is not the way to peace. It is all about surrender, and I have a feeling that this word surrender is very much at the heart of the ministry of healing. I don't need to know everything, and to use Baxter's words at the end of the hymn:

> But 'tis enough that Christ knows all
> And I shall be with him.

The hope of heaven is in itself a healing influence in our lives. There is one reading I love to hear at a funeral service, and it is from Revelation 21:2–4:

> 'See, the home of God is among mortals.
> He will dwell with them;
> they will be his peoples,
> and God himself will be with them;
> he will wipe away every tear from their eyes.
> Death will be no more;
> mourning and crying and pain will be no more,
> for the first things have passed away.'

These words have brought immeasurable comfort to me in my times of grieving. Not only is it a great comfort to know that the days of pain and suffering have come to an end for the friend who has suffered and died, but I know that in the plan of God there will come a day when at last 'the first things' will be ended. The time of these first things contains so much suffering and pain, but in the age to come they will be gone for ever, as God comes to dwell with us. This is indeed a hope for the future, but we are not to compartmentalise it away to the future. We have to own it now, and know that every time we welcome God to make his home with us, there is a measure of the healing of heaven given to us now. It may come as a miraculous cure; it may come as the visit of a friend; it may come as a word in season; it may come in the sound of music. At the heart of this healing journey is the welcoming of Jesus to my wounded place, so that the Kingdom of Heaven may be at work within me.

The man who thought he knew God

The man who thought he knew God crouched down and dipped his hand into the fast-running water. He felt the mud squeeze between his toes and he thought of all the rain that had fallen in the past two days. He remembered the look on the people's faces as the skies unburdened their much longed for treasure and Efah was one of the first to dance in the puddles. She had sung a hymn in her own language, the music of which sounded familiar. Paska had heard the cry of his people. Paska – this strange sheep god, this false god, this sheep idol that had been introduced to the people by some holy man, or not so holy man. The man who thought he knew God knew he must now help this people find the real God. It was time to tell them about Christ. He had tried so often, but somehow he could never find the words to say. Something in him seized up. It was something to do with embarrassment, with shame, and had he looked deeper in, he would have found fear. He had become weak and he did not like himself for it. Now was the time to act. Perhaps this idol was a dark idol, disguising itself as a god of light. It had fooled the villagers. It had even fooled Efah who seemed so full of luminosity. But this god had failed to heal Efah, and Christ could *heal* her. Yes, this was the time to tell her about his God, who had the power to heal, if she would only renounce her idol, Paska.

'You are thinking about God,' Efah's voice was behind him.

The man who thought he knew God felt caught out, and was annoyed with Efah. He stood up. 'Why must you . . .' he started, but then checked himself. This was not the way to behave. He had to tell Efah about his God of love.

'Yes, Efah, I am thinking about God, and I would like to tell you about my God.'

Efah looked puzzled. She was holding in her hand a stick that had floated into her feet when she was paddling in the river. Her sightless eyes looked at the man's mouth and he felt nervous. But he knew he had to be strong now to tell her the truth.

'But you don't need to tell me about your God,' said Efah, still holding her puzzled expression.

'Oh I do,' said the man, failing to hear Efah as confidence rose in him. 'You see, I believe in Jesus Christ, the Son of God.'

Efah smiled, a smile that annoyed the man again. He hated feeling annoyed with Efah, whom he had come to cherish. He hated the thought of dismantling her faith, and yet he knew God had sent him to help her, and he must tell her now about his God who could save and heal her. But Efah's smile kept gnawing away at his confidence. The smile spoke again.

'You have been with us through two new moons, and you have learned so little,' said Efah, betraying surprise and slight disappointment, but no condemnation.

'No, I have learned much, Efah. But I should have been telling you more.'

'You have told me much more than you think, but you have not listened as much as I thought you would.' A brightly coloured parrot swooped overhead, one of the many creatures that had come back to life following the rains. Its shadow flickered over Efah's face as she continued. 'You have not heard the most important thing', and as Efah said this, she bent to the ground and she ran her finger along the mud making the mark of a line. She then ran it the other way. Her eyebrows furrowed as her fingers provided her sight. The man who thought he knew God looked at the mark Efah had made in the mud and deep confusion welled up in him. He looked at the mud, and there drawn by the gentle finger of the blind girl was a picture of a cross. Surely not the Cross? For a few moments he was unable to say anything, and Efah listened to his silence. He then said, 'You have drawn . . .'

'A Cross,' Efah finished his sentence for him. 'This is where our dear Paska died', and as Efah said the simple words, the man who thought he knew God saw a bouquet of feelings in her face which included the colours of love and grief.

'Your Paska died?' said the man.

'Our Paska died,' said Efah, and the man felt nervous, and feelings of needing to put her right rose to his lips but never became words as she continued, 'As I told you, Raal listened to us for many days before he told us about Paska. He said Paska had many different names, but he waited until he felt he knew the best name to offer to us. Actually Paska is not his full name. I don't know why, but we could not say his full name easily, and Raal said that did not matter and it was probably better that we called him by our name.'

By now the dark rain-bearing clouds were lumbering away from the village to take their gifts to others. In their place, the opaque blue opened up, and the sun warmed the mud by their feet so that steam rose from the ground. The man who thought he knew God gazed at Efah, now looking like a child angel in the swirling mists around her. He knew she was saying something so important but everything in him wanted to correct her. It was almost as if a great spiritual battle was taking place. Was Efah a demon disguised as an angel of light? Was he on the verge of being fooled into adopting a pagan religion? He walked up the bank away from the river. He needed to do something to express the irritation and anxiety he felt in his soul. Efah did not move, but continued to look out over the river. She still continued to hold the stick in her hand. They had had so many conversations here in this place, but somehow the man knew this was the one that was the most important. He breathed in the now warm, damp air and looked to the blue sky. 'Help me, Lord,' he prayed, and then returned to Efah who seemed not to have noticed his temporary absence.

'So what was his full name that you could not say easily?' said the man, surprising himself that he was continuing Efah's conversation when he really wanted to follow his own.

Efah lifted her head and looked up to the man. 'His full name', she said with great gentleness, 'is the Paschal Lamb.' She said the words slowly and deliberately, her mouth needing to work hard to articulate the two Ls.

Now it was the man's turn to gaze out over the river to the wild land and mountains beyond. He wanted to speak but his thoughts had no words.

'He is our Paska,' she said and smiled and took his hand.

'Why . . . why did you not tell me this?' said the man who thought he knew God.

'Because we saw that you could not hear. I think Paska started to heal your ears when you were in the companionship room. If you had ears when you first came here, you would have heard much more. But I think Paska has helped me to be your ears.'

'Yes . . . yes,' said the man who felt he must look like an armed robber who had been stripped of his weapons. 'Tell me, Efah, why did Raal choose "Paschal Lamb" as the name to give him? You see, I know him as Jesus, as Christ, as Lord, Messiah – in fact many names.'

'Oh yes, we know all those names as well. Raal taught us much. But you see we are a people who have suffered much and have rejoiced much. Raal told us that Paska came down from heaven as the Suffering Lamb of God. The gods we worshipped before were gods that frightened us. We had to keep them happy with sacrifices. They were angry and they did not care for us. Raal told us about the Lamb of God who came as a poor man into this world, like a lamb in the midst of wild animals. He told us that he was sacrificed for us by being nailed to the Cross. We all wept when he told us that story. But then he told us that he came back to life to live forever. We were worried, because we thought he must then be a powerful god who would live in heaven and not care for us. We worried that once again we would be serving a distant angry god. But then Raal told us that a man called John, a friend of Paska, was suffering terribly but had a vision where he saw Paska, and Paska was still a lamb! Yes, he was on a throne in heaven, but he was still a lamb!' Here Efah clapped her hands and laughed, and the sunshine in her soul broke out and pushed away the lumbering cloud of confusion over the man's soul.

The man who thought he knew God talked with Efah until nightfall.

As he lay in his bed that night listening to the now familiar night-time sounds that once had scared him, he prayed to the God he shared with the people of this village. He had come to tell Efah about God, but he had discovered Efah knew and loved God in a far deeper way than he had. Efah had showed him the shallowness of his own faith, and sorrow lapped at his shore. Before he fell into a sleep of peace, he prayed that he would know God as Efah did, and during the night his prayer began to be answered in those depths only reached in the valley of dreams.

Chapter 7

The Mystery of Healing

I started writing this book on a day when I heard from Brother Ramon that he had been diagnosed with cancer. It is now eighteen months later. During these months I have witnessed a remarkable healing event in Ramon's life which has included the service of anointing with oil and the laying on of hands, together with the benefits of medicine and therapies that have combined to ensure a wonderful recovery of strength, and a year of his being largely free from pain and sickness. Also during this year he has engaged in the mystery of suffering and healing. Despite the bright light of good health, there have been moments during the year when Ramon has known shadows of pain that have reminded him of his mortality. Then, on his summer holiday, the pain intensified, and the autumn has seen a return of the cancer and an engaging in the wrestling mystery of this God who seems to be a God who sometimes heals and sometimes doesn't heal, and who at times heals for a season, then allows sickness to return. Today I write having just phoned Glasshampton Monastery and the news I hear tells me that my friend's days on earth are not likely to be many more. On New Year's Eve, when the fireworks soar into the midnight sky celebrating the new millennium, a Franciscan hermit will be preparing his soul to welcome sister death who will, at the chosen time, usher his soul into the nearer presence of Christ.

Although Brother Ramon has lived in solitude for ten years, he has a huge number of friends as is evidenced by the post which arrives at Glasshampton. All those who love him are also passing through this misty time of uncertainty and hurt, puzzling over the healing actions of God. And we are not the only ones. As I write I am close to two other people who are also battling with cancer and with the threats of untimely death that it brings. And beyond my own circle of friends there are thousands of others who wake at nights and wonder why they, or their families or friends, are suffering when they have prayed and prayed for healing and freedom from pain.

Yesterday I met Tony, a man of my age who leads one of the thriving new churches on the south coast of England. He had just flown in from Phoenix, Arizona (which made my journey from Derby look rather ordinary). He told me how he was glad to be here, a gladness which had deeper significance when he told me that two years ago he had been given only a few weeks to live as medical staff had diagnosed a fast growing cancer in his lymphatic system. He journeyed down the chemotherapy road and reviewed his life and his priorities, and he found himself being drawn ever closer to the Lord Jesus. He got to the point where he only wanted God's will, and as he put it, 'If I lived I was with Jesus, and if I died I would be with Jesus, so I couldn't lose!' The chemotherapy was given to slow down the progress of the cancer and grant him a little extra time, but to the astonishment of the doctors, Tony started to recover. In time he made a complete recovery, and there are no signs of cancer anywhere in him. Whilst he and his family are clearly overjoyed at the cure, he then told me that one of the hardest things for him was that only weeks before he was diagnosed, he had taken the funeral service of a very good friend who had died from cancer. She was a member of his church, a young mum of his age, and the church had prayed and cried out to God with every bit as much yearning and energy as they had done for Tony. As Tony recovered he had to face the painful question, 'Why did I live and she die?' I was impressed to see that he did not even attempt to answer the question.

On the occasions that I met with Ramon following the service of anointing, we often spoke of this great puzzle. The fact that some are cured and others are not can drive us to all kinds of disturbing conclusions about the nature of God. It questions his love – does he love some people more than others? Did he love Tony more than the young mum? Or is it that his power is limited? Is he powerless to do a cure in some situations? Or is it sin in our lives, or not enough prayer, or the presence of dark powers or . . . or . . . or . . .? And so it goes on, and no answer seems very satisfactory. Nine months after the healing service, Ramon wrote:

> I find it remarkable that I am in such good heart and moderate health as I write in May 1999 . . . The pain has abated with only twinges to remind me of the stark diagnosis, and I was told that I could return to gentle veggie gardening. I have been strongly sup-

ported quietly but surely by my SSF community, and by the prayers of so many people who have been sensible enough not to ring the monastery. This has increased my sense of gratitude and simple dependence, and throughout there has been a quiet joy and trust, without evading the reality of the cancer and its implications. It has been 'back to business' in almost every way, and a continuation of my life in solitude and prayer in my enclosure at Glasshampton.

At this time Ramon was also aware of episodes of niggling pain that still reminded him that the condition could return, and these reminders caused him to do characteristic deep thinking. It was his reflections on these that led him to write something that I have found so helpful:

Before the consultant session, I had prayed through these episodes, and felt the Lord say that I was demanding my kind of healing, which is 'slick, quick, charismatic and complete', and that I should rather receive the Lord's healing for me which is 'gradual, sacramental, gentle and incomplete'.

His remarks made me starkly aware of my own desire to control. Yes, I have been very guilty of demanding *my* kind of healing, a healing which conforms to my standards, a healing in which God performs according to my will and wishes. Life would be so much simpler if God was at our beck and call, but the agonising puzzles we face in the healing ministry remind us all too often that we cannot control God. In each situation we will need to listen to the voice of God. In Ramon's situation he heard a number of vital insights for his healing journey. He was learning that God's healing is never slick, and it is not often quick. Although there are many examples of dramatic and sudden cures, often healing comes gradually. We need time to allow the healing process to speak to our soul, our lifestyle, our attitudes, the quality of our relationships, our concern for the poor and so much more. We need the sacramental approach which certainly goes a long way to preventing the horror of slick techniques slipping into the healing experience. Ramon was also hearing that though he wanted the dynamic powerful charismatic force to transform his mortal body, God was dealing with him in a more gentle way. There is no healing without the power of God, and yet such power is often expressed in such gentle ways, the ways of love. The incompleteness was a puzzle to Ramon, so he explored it further:

> When I asked what 'incomplete' meant, I heard this: 'your salvation is incomplete, your sanctification is incomplete, your humanity is incomplete – until the coming of Christ, and so is this healing.'

This is the perspective of hope that we were exploring in the last chapter. Despite our best attempts to tie everything up so that it is neat and tidy, there is nothing complete in this life, and until Jesus returns, there will always be the puzzles.

Why?

The trouble with mystery is that there are no obvious answers. We can feel trapped by mystery, a sense of helplessness which feels frustrated by lack of know-ledge, insight and wisdom. There is a longing that there *must* be a solution, a final chapter in which some clever detective puts the clues together and tells us what it all means. The worst of it is that, when we are suffering and hurting, the last thing we want to be doing is to be wrestling with life's greatest mysteries. We want nice clear answers, not awkward puzzles. People often ask 'why?' in the face of tragedy, and often close behind that 'why?' is a deep sense of anger that no one has given a good and simple answer. The 'why?' is put out more as a statement than a question. Reworded it might read: 'God, whoever you are, we know you are not pre-pared to give an answer to our question of why she had to die so young, but we want you to know we resent you for keeping these answers hidden from us and we think it thoroughly unfair that you should do terrible things without giving reasons for them.'

As I write, I find I'm getting stuck. I can't get past this problem. Some are cured and some are not. Yes, Brother Ramon has helped me a lot, but why, oh why, is he not cured and another friend, Tony, is cured? It would actually be easier if God did not cure anybody. The problem of suffering is bad enough, but it is made worse by the fact that God demonstrates so clearly that he *can* alleviate suffering very wonderfully and dramatically, but only in *some* circumstances. And so down the dark spiral we go again, and whilst clever people can come up with complex attempts to explain why a good and powerful God cures some people and not others, the rest of us find ourselves nervously biting our fingernails, trusting with childlike faith yet inwardly uncertain which way the divine vote will go.

At times like this I find myself sliding into one of my favourite New Testament passages and it is in Paul's letter to the Romans. We have already had a look at chapter 7 where Paul is so honest about his wrestling with the potential pitfalls of his own humanity. Chapter 8 begins with the deep cry of thankfulness that in God there is no condemnation. It then goes on to speak about the Holy Spirit, this powerful influence in our lives. This is the third person of the Trinity who is so powerful that he raised Jesus from the dead (v. 10). No power the world has ever made has been able to bring the dead back to life. But not only does the Spirit communicate the power of God, he also communicates the love of God. 'For all who are led by the Spirit of God are children of God' (v. 14). It is the Spirit who communicates to us this extraordinary reality that we are like infants on God's knee – we experience the kind of affectionate love that is enjoyed between a good father and his child.

So if we are wrestling with issues to do with the power and love of God we find ourselves in the arena of the Spirit, and Paul in Romans 8 helps us to catch something of what this means. Interestingly, the experience of knowing the power and love of God does not take us away from all suffering. This is what Paul says,

> ... it is that very Spirit bearing witness with our spirit that we are children of God, and if children, then heirs, heirs of God and joint heirs with Christ –

> if, in fact, we suffer with him so that we may also be
> glorified with him. (v. 16)

The experience of being children, far from freeing us from all suffering, may cause us to suffer with Christ who was glorified through his suffering.

Paul could then hear people complaining about this suffering part of it all, so he goes on,

> I consider that the sufferings of this present time are not worth comparing with the glory about to be revealed to us. (v. 18)

He invites the readers to bring into the picture the eternal dimension. He is telling us that the only way to begin to make sense of the suffering of this broken world is to have one eye on the world that is to come. This could so easily be seen as escapism, but it is only escapist if there is a denial of our humanity. Our God-created humanity has this extraordinary capacity, on the one hand, to feel so acutely the pains of this mortal life, yet on the other hand to see visions of another world that not only sustain us in our suffering, but also give us hope that one day the suffering will be part of the making of a better world.

It is the suffering rooted in the experience of the cross. It is this spirituality that is so distinctive in the American Negro spirituality which produced such wonderful hymns that were sung under the scorching sun in the plantations. It is this spirituality that eventually rose above suffering slavery and racial prejudice in the 1960s and expressed itself so eloquently in the voice of Dr Martin Luther King Jr as he addressed a massive crowd of 250,000 people in Washington DC on a hot August day in 1963. Abandoning his prepared speech, he shared the dream of his heart – a dream which connected the glory of heaven to the suffering people of earth:

> I have a dream that one day every valley shall be exalted, every hill and mountain shall be made low. The rough places will be made plain and the crooked places will be made straight. This is the faith that I go back to the South with. With this faith we will be able to hew out of the mountains of despair the stone of hope. With this faith we will be able to work together, to pray together, to struggle together, to go to jail together, to stand up for freedom together, knowing we will be free one day.[1]

Corretta Scott King, writing about this famous speech in her biography of her husband, remembers,

> As Martin ended, there was the awed silence that is the greatest tribute an orator can be paid. And then a tremendous crash of sound as 250,000 people shouted in ecstatic accord with his words. The feeling that they had of oneness and unity was complete. They kept on shouting in one thunderous voice, and for that brief moment the Kingdom of God seemed to have come on earth.[2]

Seeped in the spirituality of his ancestors, Martin Luther King had grasped the meaning of this passage of St Paul, and it inspired thousands and thousands to believe that the values of heaven *could* be realised on earth. But it cost him his life, a suffering that he would have said 'was not worth comparing to the glory to be revealed'.

Returning to Paul's letter, he goes on:

> For the creation waits with eager longing for the revealing of the children of God; for the creation was subjected to futility, not of its own will but by the will of the one who subjected it, in hope that the creation itself will be set free from its bondage to decay and will obtain the freedom of the glory of the children of God. We know that the whole creation has been groaning in labour pains until now; and not only the creation, but we ourselves, who have the first fruits of the Spirit, groan inwardly while we wait for adoption, the redemption of our bodies. For in hope we were saved. Now hope that is seen is not hope. For who hopes for what is seen? But if we hope for what we do not see, we wait for it with patience. Likewise the Spirit helps us in our weakness; for we do not know how to pray as we ought, but that very Spirit intercedes with sighs too deep for words. And God, who searches the heart, knows what is the mind of the Spirit, because the Spirit intercedes for the saints according to the will of God. (Romans 8:19–27)

Paul now explores this creation and he is fascinated by the interaction of creation, the Spirit and the Spirit-filled believers. Three times in this passage he uses the Greek word *stenazo*, which describes the pain that a woman experiences during childbirth. It conveys the sense that the suffering may be very painful indeed, but it is *pro-*

ductive suffering. It will produce life, and so it is filled with hope.

Paul tells us that creation groans in labour pains, longing to see the children of God (v. 22). The children of God are the believers who have been made aware by the Spirit of God that they are his children. It is they who can bring healing to broken creation. No wonder creation aches to see them. But we who are engaged in ministering the power and love of Christ into broken creation also experience the same labour pains (v. 23). We are aching because we are engaged in broken creation. We are also aching because we know we are not yet complete – we are still waiting for, longing for, the 'redemption of our bodies', yes these wild beast bodies that one day will be transformed into resurrection bodies. It is these bodies that will fully understand, and that will be fully healed in a fully healed creation. And yet, we can know some of that fullness and healing now, because we have been given the first fruits of the Spirit. The main part belongs to heaven, but the first fruits are given now.

Then finally, and perhaps most remarkably, Paul tells us in verse 26 that the Spirit groans within us as he intercedes. In other words, as the Spirit fills us, he communicates to us the experience of groaning pain that is felt in the heart and mind of God. In this passage we see that heaven and earth, via the intermediaries of Spirit-filled believers, are joined together in this experience of shared suffering that is also closely connected with shared hope. This is why Paul can finish the chapter on such a note of triumph. 'Who can separate us from the love of Christ?' (v. 35) No one and nothing can take from us the most essential thing – the fact that we are loved by God. Thus Paul answers his question with joyful confidence, 'Nothing will be able to separate us from the love of God in Christ Jesus our Lord' (v. 39).

Beloved of God

This takes us back to the baptism of our Lord in the Jordan before the wilderness temptations, to the moment when the heavens were torn open and the voice from heaven proclaimed, 'You are my beloved Son'. No severe temptation nor ravaging wild beast, nor fierce assault by Satan could separate him from the love of God. It was this that sustained him and enabled him to walk through the dark valleys of suffering. This is our security as we journey through the painful mysteries of healing. We who love God are called to minister his healing love to a very torn and wounded world. We do not do it by trimming ourselves up to become mighty spiritual superheroes who can conquer any illness with our words of command. We do not do it by developing weird and wonderful techniques that serve to limit the grace of God only to those in the know. We do not do it by becoming healing experts who provide healing to sick clients. Neither do we do it by shrugging our shoulders in a fatalistic despair, believing in a divine lottery that cures some and fails to cure others. We do it by encountering the love of God in the wilderness of our own hearts where we meet with both the wild beasts and the angels.

I have not been able to provide a useful formula for understanding the curious mysteries in this healing ministry. I am unable to produce a checklist that we can go through when cure does not happen. I have not tried to provide excuses for a God who appears to favour some with cure whilst ignoring the cries of others. I hope I have acknowledged that in our walk with God we must begin by an honest owning of our humanity, with all its good and its bad. By following the example of our Lord Jesus, we too have to make our Spirit-led journeys into the wilderness where we become acquainted with the wild beasts without and within, and also with the divine resources of grace that empower, sustain and heal us. In such wildernesses we become aware of the possibilities of Paradise, that garden of hope that is full of the fragrance of eternity. From this garden occupied by the risen ascended Lord who still bears the marks of his suffering comes the wind of the Spirit, sometimes powerful, sometimes gentle, usually mysterious, but always warm with the love of God.

Perhaps this is where we have to leave it. We have been discovering that the healing ministry is not a bolt-on extra to the pastoral ministry of Christian people. It has to be rooted deep in our spirituality which is part of our full humanity. In fact the issue of healing takes us right into the profound mysteries of suffering that are at the heart of our humanity. The only way to be engaged in such ministry therefore is to begin by being prepared to explore the land of wild beasts and angels, within and without.

We and our friends and our families continue as pilgrims in this world of many valleys, and we know that we face now, and will face in the future, many times when the wild beasts of fear, pain, anger, injustice and sorrow, to name but a few, will make us all too aware of our vulnerability. But as we journey on, we do so as hopeful pilgrims, knowing that ultimately we will reach a promised land of solved riddles and cherished peace, where the labour pains of this world will produce such life as has never been imagined. On the journey, we are sustained by the angels, those signs of heaven breaking in, who release to us the power of God. Most crucially, we are sustained by the knowledge that only the Spirit can give, that we, struggling mortals, are held secure in the all-embracing love of Father, Son and Holy Spirit. Such knowledge does not provide slick and easy answers, but it does give us a home in which to dwell, wherein we can know the healing company of the wounded Lamb of God. In such company all of us may offer and receive the compassionate, gentle and powerful healing grace of God.

Story part 7:

The man beloved of God

The man beloved of God looked upon his Ford Sierra. It was surrounded by a crowd of laughing children. Like him, the car was repaired. It would now take him on a long journey down sandy tracks, onto major roads, on, on through many borders to his home in his cool land. He looked at the car and noticed how different he felt towards it. He thought about his three-piece suite that he had bought for less than £2000 in a grand sale; he thought about his microwave oven that had saved him so much time, and his state-of-the-art sound system that helped him relax. He thought of the four TV sets each with a video, and he thought of his CD-ROM Internet-friendly computer which he thought had opened up the whole world to him, and he frowned with discontent. That world now seemed so small. He had travelled so far.

Tonight the villagers were giving him a farewell feast, and already the goat had been killed and was being prepared for the great meal. The man beloved of God felt alone and unsettled. He had made many friends in the past weeks, but none so close as Efah, this child who had shared such wisdom with him. He strolled along a track, where, during the rains, a heavy vehicle had gorged out a deep rut that had now hardened leaving the clear imprint of the rubber tyre. Herringbone patterns in the earth. Vehicles in a quiet village. A westerner in a foreign land. He walked, sometimes in the rut, sometimes out. He felt the unevenness – sometimes in, sometimes out. This is how it was. He had been in this village, but he was also not in it. He was not and could never be a villager, especially not now, with his Ford Sierra being returned to him. That was such a stark signal to the village of his wealth, his values, his culture. Its shiny red screamed out against the khaki wooden huts.

It no longer surprised him when Efah suddenly turned up when he was in his deepest thoughts. He watched her coming across the field holding a stick in front of her to guide her. She had heard him and she was coming towards him. He stopped and watched her careful journey towards him. It would not be long before she would become a woman. He found himself worrying about her. What would happen when she grew up? How could she earn a living as a blind person? There was no getting round this blindness. Efah was too patient with it. Her lack of distress at her blindness annoyed the man. She had been to the missionaries in the next village, but they could not help. It was these missionaries who had taken a photograph of her and put it on the Internet. Her smiling face had beamed at him through his computer screen. He could still see her and he could see the caption underneath that had read, 'This blind girl needs your help'. It told stories of children who had had their sight restored through generous gifts. He remembered his mixture of feelings including a feeling that was to do with wanting to put things right.

He cared especially for this girl, who somehow felt like a daughter, he didn't know why. These feelings had caused him to take all this time away from his work, away from his land to come and help this girl. But he hadn't helped her at all. She was still poor and she was still blind. 'This blind girl needs your help' – but he had not helped, and no one could help her see again. He was rich and he could see and he was going to leave her tomorrow. Surely, surely God had brought him all this way to give some help to her. Oh, he had learned so much; he was transformed, and he knew it. Above all he had never known such an overwhelming sense of the love of God, especially in these last few days after he had discovered he had shared the same faith as the villagers. He realised how before that extraordinary discovery he was deaf to their spiritual heart because he assumed they had the wrong religion. Once his heart was open, he had found so much.

He could now hear Efah. She was singing and the sound of her singing touched him so much that he wept. Not heart-wrenching sobs, just moisture in the eyes breaking free, symbols of his sorrow at leaving a much-loved friend.

'What is your song, Efah?' he said as she approached.

'I'm singing about the man I want to marry,' said Efah and giggled contentedly.

The man beloved of God led Efah to an abandoned ant hill and together they sat facing the mountains and feeling the warm evening sun on their backs. He thought the view was one of the most beautiful he had

*ever seen, which made him feel the pain of Efah's blind-
ness even more acutely.*

'*So tell me about this man that you want to marry.*'

'*Oh, I don't know who he is, and he may be from
another village, but I am sure he will be handsome and
very loving!*' *and again she giggled.* '*But I know what
you are thinking. You are thinking to yourself, "Poor
Efah, how she would love to be married. But what man
will want to marry a poor blind girl?"*'

'*No, I . . .*' *stuttered the man, but then owned up,* '*All
right, yes that thought had crossed my mind.*'

'*It is true, there was a time when no man would marry
a blind girl. That was in the time of the other gods,
when my people believed that blindness was sent
because of crimes committed by the person or their
family. Blindness was seen as a punishment. It was a
terrible way to live. But now it is different. You see,
Paska is wounded too, so, in a way, I am a bit like
Paska because I too am wounded.*'

'*But Efah, surely your life would be easier if you could
see.*'

'*Yes, easier, but not necessarily better.*'

'*You do believe that Paska heals, don't you?*'

'*Oh yes, Paska does heal. He has healed many people
in this village.*'

'*Have you asked him to heal you?*' *He felt bad about
asking such a personal question. He turned away from
the mountains and looked at Efah and saw her tongue
pull in her bottom lip, and for a moment her lips closed
into silence. Her sightless eyes, the subject of their
conversation, looked towards him and he saw the*

moisture in their corners and he felt bad that he had intruded too far into her privacy.

'I don't mind you asking that,' she said, and not for the first time he felt that she had seen the contours of his own soul. 'Yes, I have asked Paska to cure my eyes. We had a service and we used oil. I did hope very much that I would see again. To be honest, I was sure Paska would give me my sight back. He loved me so much, so why wouldn't he treat my eyes?'

The moisture had gathered itself into a trickle now and the man watched it make its way down either side of her nose. When it reached her lips, Efah drew the back of her hand across her face, and breathed in hard. The man beloved of God took her damp hand in his and said nothing. Efah had taught him many things, but perhaps the most important was the ability to sit at ease with a difficult unanswered question. They sat in silence until they felt the heat of the sun lessen on their backs and they knew that the shadows of the tall trees behind them were lengthening as they beckoned another dark night.

The feast took place in the companionship room and went on well into the night. There was much singing and celebration. The old man who had held the man beloved of God during that night of the drought came forward and spoke to him. As he spoke, the others became quiet. He told him how glad they were he had come to their village, and how much they had learned from him. The man beloved of God told them that the village had become for him holy ground, a place of meeting with God, and more than anything else, a place of discovering the love of God. He would take that love back in his heart to his homeland.

Before the celebration ended one of the dream listeners came to him. A lady in middle years who looked deep into his eyes. She said, 'I have seen one of your dreams. You have a brother, but that part of your heart that was made to love him has gone cold. I can see fear in your eyes as I mention him. Your heart is unhealed, but when you reach out your hand to his, to hold and to trust, then you will receive your healing. In fact, I see you are receiving your healing as we speak, for Paska is with us.' The man beloved of God was never able to describe the range of emotions that swept through him as she spoke, but as he left the companionship room, he knew that something old and frozen within him was melting. He thought of his brother now with tenderness.

'You must leave before the sun rises,' said Efah. They were standing in their favourite place by the river. They had stood so often here and discussed so many things and shared so many feelings.

'Efah, why must I leave before the sun rises?' the man beloved of God said in a voice that was almost teasing.

'Because then your last memory of this village will be of mystery.' In the cloudless deep blue sky the new moon shone brilliantly and the thin bright reflection frisked on the water. The stars were so dense that they too could be seen flitting here and there on the face of the water, points of light, dynamic as the Spirit of God.

'Why should I leave in mystery? I have learned so much wisdom here.'

'We have learned much wisdom in this place, but we

have discovered many mysteries', and Efah was thinking especially of the mystery of her uncured eyes.

'Efah, when my car was returned, there were also some letters from my friends at home. I wanted to tell you that in one of them I heard about a man who is trying to write a book on the ministry of healing.'

'Trying to write a book on healing?' said Efah, and the man beloved of God heard the astonishment in her voice.

'Well, it's not uncommon in our land. There are many books on this subject.'

'But can you write about such things?'

'Well, this man obviously thinks he can.'

'And what does he say?' Efah's unsighted eyes looked up to the stars she could not see above her.

'I don't know, Efah, but I am told that in the last chapter he is trying to work out this mystery of why some people are cured by Paska and some are not cured.'

'He is trying to work it out? Did you say he is trying to work it out?' Efah's voice grew higher with her astonishment. Then, her wonderful smile, like the moon, shone out into the darkness, and her smile became a chuckle, and the chuckle got inside the man beloved of God, and their chuckle became laughter and their laughter ran down the bank into the river and across over the plains, into the mountains and up, up into the night sky joining the stars, galaxies and the thin contented moon.

Notes

Chapter 1: Following Jesus

1. David Watson, *Fear No Evil* (Hodder and Stoughton, 1984).
2. David Bannerman, *The Birds of the British Isles* Vol. 8 (Oliver and Boyd), p. 357.

Chapter 2: Healing and Humanity

1. For a fuller account of this debate, see J.N.D. Kelly's *Early Christian Doctrines* (A&C Black, 1958), ch. 13. Pelagius has traditionally been regarded as the heretic of the piece, giving rise to the heresy called 'Pelagianism'.
2. See, for example, Michele Guinness, *A Little Kosher Seasoning* (Hodder and Stoughton, 1998).
3. John Woolmer, *Healing and Deliverance* (Monarch, 1999).
4. Michael Green, *Matthew for Today* (Hodder and Stoughton, 1988), p. 98.
5. Samual Solivan, *The Spirit, Pathos and Liberation – Toward an Hispanic Pentecostal Theology* (Sheffield Academic Press, 1998).
6. ibid., pp. 11f.
7. David Runcorn, *Rumours of Life* (DLT, 1996), p. 72.

Chapter 3: The Value of the Sick

1. Michael Mitton, *The Wisdom to Listen* (Grove Pastoral Series No. 5, 1981).

2. Christian Listeners offers training in listening skills at various levels. There are regional staff in Scotland, Wales, England and the Republic of Ireland who are willing to set up training events. For more details contact the Acorn Christian Foundation, Whitehill Chase, Bordon, Hants, GU35 0AP.

3. I am aware as I write that we as a society find it hard to settle on a way of describing people with mental and intellectual disabilities. I can well understand how many of the terms can be offensive and hurtful, and I am also aware that the pressures to be politically correct can almost render us wordless. So I simply plead that my sincere intention is to use terminology that values rather than devalues.

4. Jean Vanier, *Becoming Human* (DLT, 1999), p. 2.

5. Frances Young, *Encounter with Mystery – Reflections on L'Arche and Living with Disability* (DLT, 1997).

6. ibid., p. 136.

7. David Ford, *The Shape of Living* (Fount, 1997), p. 103.

Chapter 4: Listening in the Darkness

1. Augusta Theodosia Drane, 'What the Soul Desires', full version of poem in *The Oxford Book of English Mystical Verse* (1917), p. 242.

2. Morris Maddocks, *The Vision of Dorothy Kerin* (Hodder, 1991), p. 50.

3. Malidoma, *Ritual: Power, Healing and Community* (Gateway Books, 1996), p. 37.

4. For those who want to know more about the 'Toronto Blessing' see my booklet, *The Heart of Toronto* (Grove Books). In this booklet I attempt to explore what was going on in this movement. There are some very interesting parallels with Christian mysticism.

Chapter 5: Healing in the Heart of Community

1. In his Gospel Luke tells us about Jesus sending out the twelve (ch. 9) and the seventy (ch. 10). Whilst the twelve

apostles might be seen as the 'elders', the seventy can be seen as the disciples who have no leadership role as such, but who are simply called to share the good news of the Kingdom – i.e. all of us. A natural part of our proclamation of the Kingdom of God is to heal the sick (Luke 10:9).

2. In case you are wondering 'Why Rhino Club?', the answer is this: at our first meeting, which included several travelling evangelists, J. John told us that some famous evangelist had said that they needed to have the skin of a rhinoceros to survive. This led to the idea of the Rhino Club, and it was Adrian Plass who recognised immediately that these letters stood for 'Really Holy If Naughty Occasionally'. Sounds like something of wild beasts and angels in there somewhere.

3. Dietrich Bonhoeffer, *Life Together* (SCM, 1954), p. 25.

4. In *Grass Roots*, Jan/Feb 1985, pp. 12f.

Chapter 6: Healing and Hope

1. See, for example, Isaiah 40:3.

2. See Romans 5:14, 1 Corinthians 15:22, 45.

3. C. S. Lewis, *The Magician's Nephew* (Puffin, 1963), pp. 313f.

Chapter 7: The Mystery of Healing

1. Quoted in *My Life with Martin Luther King Jr* by Coretta Scott King (Hodder and Stoughton, 1969) p. 253.

2. ibid., p. 254.

Notes on the illustrations

by Lindsey Attwood

Wild Beasts and Angels deals with God embracing our humanity. The inspiration for the style of the illustrations came initially from the etchings of Rembrandt. His etchings are loosely worked sketches using light and dark to convey mood. Other influences came from the photographer Ansel Adams, whose black and white landscapes are so beautiful, and George Rouault, a Christian artist, who painted in a deeply emotive way using thick brush strokes. I have tried to capture the heart and soul expressed in each chapter with strong atmospheres, thoughtful faces, iconic images.

Chapter 1.   Jesus sits alone in the middle of nowhere, still and silent. The internal struggle begins.

Chapter 2.   Frayed at the edges. Anything but perfect. Vulnerable and needy. All of this God in Christ hugs to himself.

Chapter 3.   Matthew 6:26. Frail but infinitely valuable. Ignored or disregarded by the world, but precious in God's eyes. Jesus revolutionises our value system.

Chapter 4.   Life down in the shadows. Seeing glimpses of things that keep you going. However, we never walk alone.

Chapter 5.   Jesus at the centre of everything, in our eating, drinking, talking, in our everyday lives. The presence of Jesus defines real community.

Chapter 6. Glorified wounds. Christ is still sympathetic in heaven. The marks of his humanity continue to be seen.

Chapter 7. Mystery. The path through the maze. Living with unanswered questions. Yet nothing can separate us from the love of God.